Jane

Jane Snow Cooks
Spirited Recipes and Stories

Jane Snow

Ringtaw Books Akron, Ohio

13   12   11   10   09   5   4   3

LIBRARY OF CONGRESS CATALOGING-IN-PUBLICATION DATA

Snow, Jane, 1949–
  Jane Snow cooks : spirited recipes and stories / Jane Snow. — 1st ed.
    p. cm.
  ISBN 978-1-931968-65-2 (pbk. : alk. paper)
  1. Cookery, American. 2. Cookery—Ohio—Akron. I. Title.
  TX715.S677 2009
  641.59771'36—dc22
                        2009030573

The paper used in this publication meets the minimum requirements of American National Standard for Information Sciences—Permanence of Paper for Printed Library Materials, ANSI Z39.48–1984. ∞

Articles reprinted with permission of the *Akron Beacon Journal* and Ohio.com.

Cover design and image by Garrett Haas.

The interior was designed and typeset by Amy Freels, with help from Amanda Gilliland. The type was set in Futura. The interior illustrations are by Amanda Gilliland. The book was printed and bound by BookMasters of Ashland, Ohio.

Contents

Acknowledgments

Most of the recipes in this book originally appeared under my byline in the *Akron Beacon Journal* from 1982 to 2006. A heartfelt thank you to the newspaper for allowing me to reprint them.

Thanks especially to Bruce Winges, Stuart Warner and four extraordinary editors: Ann Sheldon Mezger, Michelle LeComte, Barbara Griffin and Jan Leach. I am forever grateful for your patience, encouragement and advice.

Foreword

I know reporters who dodged bullets in Vietnam. One former colleague joined the Ku Klux Klan undercover to get a story. Others have braved fire, floods and hurricanes.

I, too, have faced danger in the pursuit of journalism. In December of 1990, Jane Snow led WNIR radio host Stan Piatt and I into battle. Or should I say a food fight. Staring at us that dreary afternoon were 158 fruitcakes. ONE HUNDRED AND FIFTY-EIGHT FRUITCAKES! Were we nuts? Yes, and candied cherries and chopped dates, too. We met the enemy and we swallowed him. It took all we had not to spit him back out.

More than four hours later, we declared victory. We found one fruit-cake worth eating. That recipe is in this book. The other 157 entries are still buried somewhere in the bowels of the *Beacon Journal*. I believe they have a half-life of 74 years so the building should be safe again sometime this millennium.

Why did Piatt and I put ourselves in harm's way like that? Because Jane asked.

And when the subject in Akron was food, everybody did what Jane said. We went to the restaurants she liked. We used the cooking tips she provided. We prepared the recipes she recommended. She was a community's palate for almost three decades. And we ate well. Maybe too well sometimes.

Most of you remember Jane as a food critic; I prefer to think of her as a damn fine journalist no matter what the topic she covered. She was every bit as detailed in her work as the best investigative reporters. That's why four times she was a finalist for the James Beard Award, the nation's most prestigious honor for a culinary writer, and twice a winner.

But now I have put myself in danger once again. This essay stands between you and more than 200 pages of commentary and Jane's favorite recipes. It is a virtual history book of cooking in the Akron area.

You'll learn the secret of sauerkraut balls and Canova's chili. You'll discover why folks in Barberton used to say that if the Colonel had made chicken this good, he'd have been a general. (As a native Kentuckian, I can assure you the Colonel never thought of using four pounds of lard to fry his birds. Nor serving them with hot sauce. Might have messed up his suit.)

You'll taste the red velvet cake before you even get to the cooking instructions. (I always thought the cake got its name from the wallpaper that used to hang in Casa Mimi's and so many other area restaurants.)

So I'm going to get out of your way right now, because I've seen how much you like to eat. And how surly you can be when you're hungry.

Turn the page and start cooking.

Bon appétit.

Stuart Warner is a former columnist, reporter and Pulitzer Prize-winning editor at The Beacon Journal *and* The Plain Dealer *in Cleveland.*

Introduction

Workers at a Northeast Ohio auto factory once staged a month-long protest when they couldn't get the *Akron Beacon Journal's* Food section delivered at work.

"A lot of us are bachelors," a protestor told me by phone. "We need your recipes! Other recipes are too complicated."

When my food section started arriving with the *Beacon Journal* again, the guys removed the tape from coin-box slots, but for years I kept them in mind each time I chose a recipe. It had to be delicious, of course, and clearly explained, with ingredients that weren't impossibly expensive or difficult to round up. And if I could streamline the steps or reduce the number of utensils required, I'd do it.

During my two-plus decade career as food editor of the *Akron Beacon Journal*, I printed thousands of recipes. This book is a compilation of the very best—a one-of-a-kind collection of great-tasting, user-friendly recipes, many of them with a uniquely local flavor.

In these pages you'll find the storied cheesecake recipe from Lou & Hy's Deli, the delicate Almond Crèmes that beat out hundreds of other entries in a holiday cookie contest, and a grilled chicken recipe that brought my friends to their knees.

To track down recipes, I scoured restaurant kitchens and food factories, interviewed hundreds of chefs and home cooks and judged recipe contests galore. When I couldn't find a recipe my readers wanted, I created one myself. That's how I was able to share recipes for the legendary Cannova's Chili, Ken Stewart's white French dressing and Barberton Fried Chicken.

Along with those recipes and more, I've included stories about eating my way through Ohio and beyond. On one memorable road trip, I cooked a 2½-pound roast on the manifold of a car (it tasted awesome). On a journey to France, I ate every item sold in a tiny bakery in the Loire Valley, then returned home and recreated the pastries in my kitchen. The recipe for a custard-filled brioche from that trip is in this book.

I occasionally wandered far afield in search of recipes and trends. I interviewed a sun-weathered barbecue expert in a field in South Carolina, a hazelnut farmer in a grove in Oregon, and a New Orleans chef on a riverboat over a plate of crawfish. They all had stories to tell and recipes to share. Many of the recipes have remained favorites. An explosively flavored lemon-walnut chicken salad from chef Joyce Goldstein in San Francisco is still the best I've tasted, and I know I'll never find a better recipe for crab cakes than the one I got in Baltimore.

But still, there's no place like home. Where else in the world can you find hot rice, sauerkraut balls and kidney bean salad, sometimes all at the same meal?

These foods are woven into the culinary fabric of the Akron area, and for more than two decades I had the time of my life sharing them with you. It's a joy to share them with you once again.

Jane Snow Cooks

The Recipes

Chapter 1
Local Favorites

J ust as the rubber industry shaped the Akron area's history, the quirky local foods consumed by workers and burghers alike have helped shape its personality.

A citizenry has to have a sense of humor to name a deep-fried nugget of breaded sauerkraut its official food, as residents did in a regional vote in 1996.

An independent streak is required to think of kidney bean salad as one of the major food groups. The mayonnaise, relish and bean mixture is found on restaurant menus across the region and on picnic tables in parks and backyards.

And how about the way we cling to Art's bean soup and Kaase's creamed chicken in a potato basket decades after the restaurants have closed? We're either loyal or stubborn, take your pick.

These and many other unique foods are woven into the region's culinary fabric, contributing their flavor notes to the richness and diversity of the local culture. Where else in the world can you find Barberton chicken, hot rice or Cannova's chili?

We still relish the devil dogs sold from bakery trucks in the 1950s, and we've never gotten over our fascination with red velvet cake—or, unfortunately, those miniature meatballs simmered in grape jelly. But we won't go there.

This chapter celebrates the foods that define our region, from Waterloo Restaurant's glorious coconut-cream pie with its tender-crumbly crust to the tart-sweet coleslaw we serve with fried chicken.

If you've ever yearned for one more hunk of Budd's banana-pineapple cake or a bowl of Bangkok Gourmet's suave coconut-Siamese ginger soup, dig in.

Coconut-Siamese Ginger Soup

Coconut milk, lime and chicken broth form the backbone of an explosively flavored soup that's a bit exotic yet deeply comforting. The soup was wildly popular at Akron's first Thai restaurant, Bangkok Gourmet. Chef-owner Sue Fogle shared the recipe.

2 (14-ounce) cans coconut milk
(not coconut cream)

½ stalk lemon grass, cut into 1-inch pieces

3 kaffir lime leaves

2 pieces (1-inch long) Siamese
ginger, peeled

2 tablespoons Thai chili paste

10 ounces boneless chicken breasts,
sliced into bite-sized pieces

½ cup canned straw mushrooms

2 cups chicken broth

½ teaspoon salt, or to taste

1 tablespoon nam pla (fish sauce), or to taste

Lime juice

Coriander leaves, green onions and
red-hot Thai chili powder for garnish

Bring coconut milk to a boil in a large saucepan. Add lemon grass, lime leaves, Siamese ginger and chili paste. Stir well, reduce heat and simmer for 15 minutes. Add chicken, mushrooms, chicken broth, salt and fish sauce. Simmer 10 minutes longer.

To serve, ladle soup into bowls. Add a dash of lime juice (about ½ teaspoon) to each portion. Top with a sprinkling of chopped coriander leaves and green onions. Add a pinch of Thai chili powder if more heat is wanted.

Nick Anthe's Bean Salad

Kidney bean salad is an Akron thing, like sauerkraut balls and beets on salads. At least a half-dozen local restaurants, from Nick Anthe's to Papa Joe's, serve it as a pre-dinner snack, and it is as popular with home cooks as it is with chefs. The basic salad is canned kidney beans and finely diced onion dressed with mayonnaise. Variations abound, but this one is considered the original.

 5 cups cooked red kidney beans
 ¾ cup diced celery
 ¾ cup diced Spanish onions
 1 cup diced sweet pickles
 ½ teaspoon salt
 1 teaspoon white pepper
 ½ cup mayonnaise (or to taste)
 2 tablespoons sweet pickle juice

Rinse beans thoroughly and drain very well. Mix with all other ingredients. Chill.

Makes about 15 servings.

Waterloo Coconut-Cream Pie

The pastry for the world-class pies at Waterloo Restaurant in south Akron is still rolled out one disk at a time and baked daily, as it has been since 1957. The owners shared the recipe for the filling but not the top-secret recipe for the crust, so I tinkered with ingredients to find a formula that comes close. The pastry is tender and crumbly rather than flaky. With the slightest pressure of a fork, the crust falls away in buttery chunks. The coconut cream filling is one of the restaurant's most popular.

Cookie-like crust

2 cups flour

¼ cup sugar

1 teaspoon salt

¾ cup chilled lard

2 tablespoons cold butter

1 egg

¼ cup milk

Coconut Filling

2 boxes (4 serving size) vanilla pudding mix (not instant)

3 tablespoons coconut flavoring

1 cup frozen whipped topping, thawed

½ cup shredded coconut, lightly toasted

¼ cup blanched slivered almonds, lightly toasted

2 (9-inch) baked pie shells

Additional whipped topping, toasted coconut, toasted almonds for garnish

Crust: Whisk together flour, sugar and salt in a medium bowl. Add lard and butter in chunks. With a pastry blender, cut fats into flour until bits are about the size of peas.

Beat egg and milk together. Drizzle over flour mixture, tossing with a fork. Gather into a ball and knead briefly with hands. Wrap and chill for at least 30 minutes.

Divide dough in half. On a well-floured board, roll one portion of dough into a 12-inch circle. Ease into a 9-inch pie pan. For an unbaked pie shell, crimp edges and prick dough all over with a fork. Repeat with remaining dough. Bake at 450 degrees for about 20 minutes, until the centers begin to brown. Cool completely before filling.

Makes 2 pie shells or 1 double-crust pie.

Filling: Prepare both boxes of pudding according to package directions. Chill several hours or overnight.

Several hours before serving, place pudding in a mixer bowl and beat until smooth and fluffy. Fold in coconut flavoring and the 1 cup whipped topping. Gently fold toasted coconut and almonds into filling.

Pour filling into baked pie shells. Swirl whipped topping over filling and lightly sprinkle with toasted coconut and almonds, if desired. Chill thoroughly.

Makes 2 pies.

Note: Toast coconut and nuts by spreading on separate baking sheets and baking at 350 degrees just until coconut begins to turn golden, and for nuts, for about 3 to 4 minutes, until they're crisp but have not changed color.

Chicken in a Nest

Decades after Kaase's restaurant closed in downtown Akron, the creamed chicken in a potato basket remains popular. The potato baskets are made by clamping raw shoestring potatoes in a bird's-nest fryer and lowering into a deep fryer. The gadget is sold at cookware and some hardware stores. Two long-handled metal strainers 4 inches in diameter are a good substitute.

Potato nests

5 baking potatoes
4 cups peanut oil for deep frying

Creamed chicken filling

3 tablespoons butter
6 tablespoons flour
1 cup chicken broth
1 cup half and half
¾ pound cooked chicken meat, diced
Salt, fresh-ground pepper
Chopped parsley for garnish

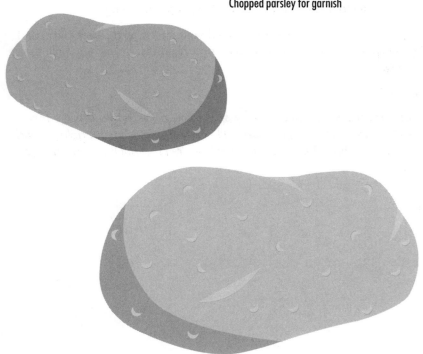

Nests: Peel the potatoes and grate them coarsely. As you do this, keep the grated potato in lightly salted water so it will not discolor. Press the grated potatoes dry on paper towels.

Heat the oil in a deep fryer or deep pan to 380 degrees. Dip a bird's-nest frying basket into the pan to oil it.

Take the baskets apart and fill the bottom basket with the grated potatoes, forming a basket of potato within the wire basket. Replace the smaller basket within the larger and clamp shut. Deep-fry until golden brown, about 3 minutes.

To remove, gently take out the smaller basket. Knock out the potato basket by gently tapping the wire frame upside down on the counter. The potato basket will fall out. Drain on paper towels.

Filling: In a medium saucepan, melt the butter. Add the flour and whisk and stir over medium-low heat for 1 to 2 minutes. Do not brown. Raise heat to medium-high. Whisk in the chicken broth and half and half. Bring to a simmer, whisking until smooth. Stir in the cooked chicken and warm through. Season to taste with salt and pepper.

Arrange potato baskets on a platter or 8 plates and fill them with the hot chicken filling. Garnish with chopped parsley.

Makes 8 baskets.

Cranberry Velvet

This Akron Thanksgiving favorite isn't haute cuisine—it's made with miniature marshmallows, crushed pineapple and canned cranberry sauce—but just try leaving it off the Thanksgiving table. When I mentioned it in a column once, more than 100 recipes poured in.

2 cups miniature marshmallows
1 (16-ounce) can whole cranberry sauce
1 cup crushed pineapple, drained
2 tablespoons lemon juice
Pinch of salt
1 cup whipping cream, whipped

Combine marshmallows, cranberry sauce, pineapple, lemon juice and salt. Fold in whipped cream. Chill overnight in refrigerator.

Makes 6 to 8 servings.

Chicken House Coleslaw

Serving Barberton chicken without a pile of crisp, refreshing slaw on the side would be unthinkable. The slaw is tart, thanks to the vinegar-based dressing.

2 cups shredded cabbage

⅓ cup sliced green pepper

¼ cup chopped parsley

3 tablespoons vinegar

2 tablespoons sugar

2 tablespoons vegetable oil

1 teaspoon salt

In bowl, combine cabbage, green pepper and parsley. Combine vinegar, sugar, oil and salt and stir until sugar is dissolved. Pour over slaw and toss. Cover and chill. Stir again just before serving.

Makes 5 to 6 servings.

Chicken House Hot Rice

Whether you call it hot rice or hot sauce, this unusual rice side dish is as common as salt and pepper in Barberton chicken houses. The rice is cooked with tomatoes and spiced up with paprika and a hot pepper.

2 onions, chopped

1 fresh hot pepper, such as a Hungarian wax pepper, sliced

2 tablespoons butter

Paprika to taste

2 (16-ounce) cans stewed tomatoes

½ cup long grain uncooked white rice

Salt, pepper

Brown onions and sliced pepper in the butter in a medium saucepan. Add paprika to taste.

Process tomatoes briefly in blender. Add tomatoes, rice, salt and pepper to pan. Cover and cook over low heat until rice is tender and the liquid has been absorbed, about 20 minutes. Remove pepper slices before serving.

Jane Snow Cooks

Art's Place Bean Soup

Although both Art's Place restaurants are gone, the popular '70s and '80s eateries live on in kitchens across Northeast Ohio through this popular soup. A big bowlful will warm any winter day. Serve it with squares of cornbread, as Art's did.

1 pound dry navy beans
2 quarts cold water
4 smoked ham hocks
½ teaspoon salt
6 whole peppercorns
1 bay leaf
1 medium onion, sliced
Salt, pepper

Wash beans, place in heavy soup pot, and cover with cold water. Bring to a boil and boil for 2 minutes. Remove from heat, cover, and let stand 1 hour.

Add ham hocks, salt, peppercorns and bay leaf. Add more water to cover ham hocks, if necessary. Cover pan, bring to a boil, and simmer gently until beans are tender, about 3 hours. Add onion during last 30 minutes of cooking time.

Remove ham hocks, shred meat and return meat to soup. Mash a few of the beans with potato masher to thicken soup. Season to taste with salt and pepper.

Makes 6 servings.

Rum Cream Pie

Those of you who remember the Smorgasbord in Stow probably remember the restaurant's rum cream and sour cream raisin pies. The pies were so good that the recipes were included in an old Duncan Hines cookbook. They're still remembered fondly by old-timers and by anyone who makes and tastes the pies.

6 egg yolks
1 cup sugar
1 tablespoon unflavored gelatin
½ cup cold water
2 cups heavy (whipping) cream
½ cup dark rum
1 10-inch baked pie shell
Shaved bittersweet chocolate

Beat egg yolks with a mixer until lemon-colored and thick. Slowly beat in sugar. In a small saucepan, soak gelatin in cold water until softened, then bring to a boil over low heat. Slowly pour over sugar-egg mixture, stirring briskly to prevent eggs from curdling.

Whip cream until stiff. Fold into pie filling. Add rum and stir well. Cool but do not let set. Pour into a 10-inch baked pie shell. Sprinkle generously with shaved bittersweet chocolate. Chill until set.

Note: This filling contains raw eggs. To reduce the risk of food-borne illness, use pasteurized eggs.

Sour Cream Raisin Pie

The ultimate raisin pie recipe comes from the former Smorgasbord in Stow.

½ cup raisins
½ cup nuts
1 cup plus 6 tablespoons sugar
2½ tablespoons flour
1 teaspoon cinnamon
¼ teaspoon ground cloves
1½ cups sour cream
3 eggs, separated
1 10-inch baked pie shell

Chop raisins and nuts and mix together. In a medium bowl, combine 1 cup sugar, flour, cinnamon and cloves and toss with chopped raisins and nuts. Stir in sour cream and transfer to double boiler. Cook over hot water until mixture begins to bubble, then add egg yolks gradually, whisking constantly. Cook and stir until thickened. Cool, then pour into pie shell.

Beat egg whites until frothy. Add 6 tablespoons sugar gradually, beating until stiff peaks form. Top chilled pie with meringue, completely covering filling. Bake at 350 degrees for about 5 minutes, until meringue begins to brown. Cool. Dip a sharp knife in hot water before cutting.

Banana-Pineapple Cake

Those who miss the banana-pineapple cake from Budd's Bakery can console themselves with this recipe. It isn't Budd's, but it's close. The moist banana layer cake is sandwiched with a thick pineapple filling and covered with an airy seafoam frosting.

1 (18½-ounce) box yellow cake mix (no oil or pudding)
⅛ teaspoon baking soda
2 eggs
¾ cup cola
1 cup mashed ripe bananas
2 teaspoons lemon juice
⅓ cup finely chopped nuts, optional
Pineapple filling (recipe follows)
Seafoam frosting (recipe follows)

In a large mixing bowl, combine cake mix, baking soda and eggs. Measure cola, then stir briskly until foaming stops. Add to batter. Blend ingredients just until moistened, then beat at high speed with an electric mixer for 3 minutes, scraping bowl often.

Combine mashed bananas with lemon juice. Add to cake batter with nuts. Beat 1 minute at medium speed. Pour into two greased and floured, 9-inch-round cake pans. Bake at 350 degrees for about 30 minutes or until a toothpick inserted in center comes out clean. Cool in pans for 5 minutes, then remove and place right-side up on racks to finish cooling. When cool, place one layer on a serving plate, flat side up. Top with pineapple filling. Top with remaining cake layer. Frost with seafoam frosting.

Jane Snow Cooks

Pineapple Filling

½ cup sugar

4 tablespoons flour

⅛ teaspoon salt

1 egg

1 cup drained crushed pineapple

¾ cup pineapple juice

1 tablespoon butter

Combine all ingredients except butter in a heavy saucepan and stir until smooth. Cook over medium-low heat, stirring often, until mixture has thickened. Stir in butter. Remove from heat and cool. Spread between cake layers.

Seafoam Frosting

2 egg whites

1½ cups packed light brown sugar

⅛ teaspoon cream of tartar or 1 tablespoon light corn syrup

⅓ cup cola

1 teaspoon vanilla extract

Dash of salt

In top of double boiler, combine all ingredients except vanilla and beat 1 minute at high speed of electric mixer. Place over simmering water (water should not touch bottom of top pan); beat on high speed about 7 minutes, until frosting forms peaks when beater is raised.

Remove from heat and add vanilla. Continue beating on high speed until thick enough to spread, about 2 minutes. Spread on sides and top of banana cake.

Galatoboureko (custard-filled phyllo)

Some of my most treasured recipes are those for the Greek pastries sold at the annual bake sale at Annunciation Greek Orthodox Church in Akron. The members of the church's Philoptochos Society kindly shared their heirloom recipes, and this is my favorite.

5 cups milk

½ cup farina cereal

Pinch of salt

½ cup (1 stick) butter, softened

7 eggs, separated, at room temperature

¾ cup sugar

1½ teaspoons vanilla extract

16 sheets phyllo dough

½ pound butter, melted

Syrup

2½ cups water

1½ cups sugar

2 2-inch strips lemon peel

1 tablespoon fresh lemon juice

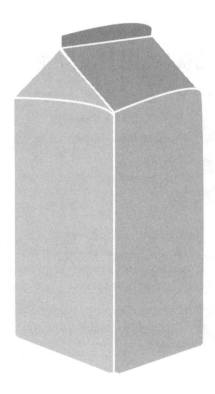

Warm milk in a large saucepan. Slowly add farina and salt, stirring constantly until thick and smooth. Remove from heat and stir in the softened butter until melted.

In a bowl, beat egg yolks with sugar until light and creamy. Slowly add to milk mixture and return to low heat. Cook and stir until thick and smooth; add vanilla. Remove from heat and place a buttered sheet of waxed paper directly on surface of custard. Cool. Beat egg whites until stiff. Fold into cooled custard. Set aside.

Layer the bottom of a 13-by-9-inch pan with eight phyllo sheets, brushing the top of each sheet with melted butter after placing in the pan. (Keep sheets covered with a damp towel until ready to use to prevent drying out.) Pour custard into pastry-lined pan. Top with remaining eight phyllo sheets, buttering as before.

Using a sharp knife, cut the top layers of phyllo lengthwise into strips 1½ inches wide. Bake at 350 degrees for 45 to 50 minutes or until golden. Let stand 5 minutes.

For the syrup: While pastry bakes, combine water and sugar in a saucepan. Bring to a boil. Simmer 20 minutes, or until candy thermometer registers 224 degrees. Add lemon peel and lemon juice and simmer 5 minutes more. Pour syrup over warm pastry. Cool completely, then cut into diamonds or squares.

Makes about 24 bars.

Kaase's Cinnamon Star Cookies

Kaase's bakery, an Akron institution for decades, provided this cookie recipe for a fan who remembered them from his childhood in the 1940s. Cinnamon stars are a traditional German Christmas treat.

¾ cup granulated sugar

1½ cups margarine

¾ teaspoon salt

2 teaspoons cinnamon

1 teaspoon vanilla extract

1½ teaspoons maple flavoring

2 eggs

3 cups all-purpose flour

1½ cups walnuts, chopped

Cinnamon sugar

Cream together the first four ingredients. Add vanilla and maple flavoring to taste. Add eggs and mix until smooth. Stir in flour and walnuts and mix until smooth. Roll out dough on floured surface and cut with a miniature star cookie cutter. Sprinkle with cinnamon sugar. Bake on greased cookie sheets at 350 degrees for about 8 minutes.

Makes 5 to 6 dozen cookies, depending on size of the stars.

Gus' Puffs

For years, a combination of mayonnaise, bread and Parmesan cheese was one of the most popular cocktail snacks in Akron. The mayonnaise on the bread puffs up and browns beautifully under the broiler, making for an easy but surprisingly delicious nosh. The puffs are a specialty of Gus' Chalet on Tallmadge Avenue in Akron.

4 ounces grated Parmesan cheese

2 cups mayonnaise

1½ onions, minced

1 loaf of day-old white bread

In a bowl, mix together half the cheese, the mayonnaise and the minced onion; set aside.

With a drinking glass or large cookie cutter, cut a round from each slice of bread. Place the rounds on cookie sheets and broil until toasted on one side.

Flip rounds over and spread untoasted sides with the mayonnaise mixture. Sprinkle with remaining cheese. Return to oven and broil until the puffs are golden brown.

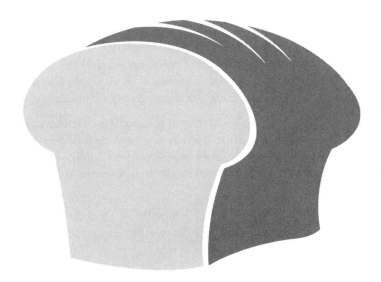

Red Velvet Cake

Although Red Velvet Cake is rumored to have been born in the South or in a hotel in New York City, the Midwest surely is where it was pensioned off. A half-century or more after its heyday, the still-vibrant beauty can be spotted all over Northeast Ohio. It is served at dozens of restaurants, from buffets to rib joints, in bakeries and by caterers, and is a staple at local weddings. This recipe is from caterer Judy Lanfranchi of Kent.

½ cup solid vegetable shortening
1½ cups sugar
2 eggs
2 tablespoons cocoa powder
2 (1-ounce) bottles red food coloring
1 cup buttermilk
1 teaspoon vanilla extract
1 teaspoon salt
2½ cups all-purpose flour
1 tablespoon distilled white vinegar
1 teaspoon baking soda

Cream shortening and sugar with an electric mixer until fluffy. Beat in eggs. In a small container, stir together cocoa and food coloring until cocoa is dissolved. Beat into creamed mixture.

Measure buttermilk and stir in vanilla and salt. Beat into cake mixture alternately with flour, in three additions each. Combine baking soda and vinegar. Add to cake batter and beat on medium speed for 2 minutes.

Pour into two greased and floured, 9-inch round cake pans. Bake at 350 degrees for 30 to 35 minutes, until cake begins to pull away from pan and top springs back when touched lightly with a finger. Remove from oven and cool 10 minutes in pans. Remove from pans and cool completely on wire racks.

Cut each layer in half horizontally. Frost and stack the four layers, then frost the sides and top. Store in the refrigerator.

Classic White Frosting

5 tablespoons flour

1 cup milk

½ cup (1 stick) butter, at room temperature

½ cup solid vegetable shortening

1 cup powdered sugar

1 teaspoon vanilla extract

Place flour in saucepan and gradually whisk in milk until smooth. Cook and stir over low heat until very thick. Cover and refrigerate until cool.

With a mixer, cream butter and shortening. Beat in sugar and vanilla until mixture looks white and fluffy. Add milk-flour mixture and continue to beat about 10 minutes, until frosting has the consistency of whipped cream.

Devil Dogs

If you call them "whoopie pies," you're not from Akron. Around here, the cream-filled chocolate snack cakes were called "devil dogs" back in the days when City Bakery trucks carried them to every neighborhood and suburb. Many locals still crave devil dogs, decades after the bakery's demise. The treats made from our recipe may not look like authentic devil dogs (they're round, not oval), but they sure taste like them.

⅔ cup solid vegetable shortening
1¼ cups sugar
2 eggs
2½ cups sifted flour
½ cup cocoa
1¼ teaspoons baking soda
¼ teaspoon cream of tartar
½ teaspoon salt
1½ teaspoons vanilla extract
1 cup milk

Filling
2 cups powdered sugar
¾ cup solid vegetable shortening
2 egg whites
¼ teaspoon salt
1 teaspoon vanilla extract

Cream together the shortening and sugar. Add eggs and beat well. Whisk together the sifted flour, cocoa, baking soda, cream of tartar and salt. Stir vanilla into the milk. Add the dry ingredients to the creamed mixture alternately with the milk in three additions each, beating after each addition.

Drop batter by tablespoons onto greased or parchment-lined cookie sheets. Bake at 375 degrees for 10 to 15 minutes. Cool, then sandwich with filling.

Filling: Place all ingredients in a bowl and beat with an electric mixer until filling stands in soft peaks. Spread some filling on the flat side of a chocolate cake. Top with the flat side of another chocolate cake. Continue with remaining cakes and filling.

Note: This filling is made with raw eggs, which could contain salmonella bacteria. The elderly and those with weakened immune systems should consider using pasteurized egg whites.

Gingerbread Molasses Cookies

For years, these crisp gingerbread cookies have been a tradition at the Ohio Mart craft fair held each fall at Stan Hywet Hall.

2 cups light molasses
2 cups sugar
1 cup margarine (not reduced-fat)
1 cup (2 sticks) butter
2 tablespoons ground ginger
4 eggs, beaten
10 cups flour

3½ teaspoons baking soda
1 teaspoon salt
½ teaspoon cinnamon
½ teaspoon nutmeg
Pinch cloves
Pinch black pepper
½ cup cold coffee

In a saucepan, combine molasses, sugar, margarine, butter and ginger. Heat until butter melts, stirring to combine. Bring to a boil and boil 1 minute. Cool to room temperature. Beat in eggs.

In a very large bowl, sift together 3 cups of the flour, baking soda, salt, cinnamon, nutmeg, cloves and pepper. Add molasses mixture and stir well to combine. Stir in coffee. Gradually stir in about 7 cups of flour, or enough to make a stiff dough.

Cover dough with plastic wrap and chill overnight. Roll dough ¼-inch thick on a floured surface and cut into circles with cookie cutters. Bake on parchment-lined baking sheets at 375 degrees for 10 minutes. Cool.

Makes 100 3-inch cookies.

The Recipes

Chapter 2
Ten Most Wanted

K en Stewart wasn't about to give me his recipe for white French salad dressing, and the recipe for Cannova's chili has been a tightly guarded secret for more than 70 years. But that didn't stop people from asking.

No, make that begging. Demands for the dressing and chili recipes clogged up my answering machine for years until I figured out a way to satisfy those requests.

It didn't take a posse to round up the 10 most-wanted recipes. All it took was some sleuthing, some cooking and the help of a few kind folks.

Some recipes I cloned, based on the flavor of the original and, in some cases, a trip to the restaurant kitchen. The recipe for Barberton chicken was pieced together during a tour of the chicken-house kitchens. The white French dressing was cloned from a sample I carted home with a carryout salad from Ken Stewart's Grille.

Other recipes—namely, Cannova's chili—took years of sleuthing to figure out and was a sensation when it was first published. The recipe can be traced to the 1930s, when chef Daddy Ross made the chili at the old Thornton Grill. Ross later cooked at Cannova's restaurant, and after his death, the recipe was passed from owner to owner.

The late Joe Messer, who owned Cannova's from 1961 to 1967, wouldn't give me the recipe, but he did give me a tub of his homemade spice mixture and told me the chili contains garlic and suet but no tomato sauce or onions.

Bits of the recipe were shared over the years by other folks who said they were Daddy Ross' milkman, or a salesman passing through the kitchen, or the hairdresser of a friend of the Cannova family. I put all of the bits together to create, finally, the real thing. I tested it on a Cannova's chili addict who doted on it for years. He took one bite and said excitedly, "You did it! This is it!"

Other recipes in this chapter were so popular that printing them didn't stop the phone calls. In this category are such blockbusters as Lou & Hy's cheesecake, roast prime rib in a salt crust, and the ginger salad dressing recipe that came from a friend of a friend of a waiter at a Japanese restaurant.

All of these recipes are treasures that have become woven into the culinary fabric of the Akron area. They're here together, in one place, for your convenience.

Now stop calling!

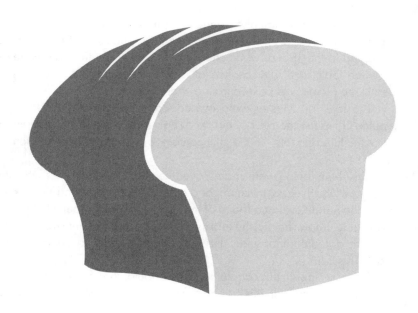

Friendship Starter

For at least 15 years, not a month went by without a request for this recipe. The starter—also called "Herman" and "Amish" starter—is a bubbling mass of yeast, flour and sugar that is "fed" with more flour and sugar every five to seven days. One to three cups must be removed regularly and either used or given to a friend—hence the name. If you run out of willing friends, freeze the starter until you're ready to bake again. Thaw it at room temperature for about 3 hours before using it in a recipe. Recipes we've printed for baked goods made with the starter are available in the science and technology division of the Akron-Summit County Public Library.

2 envelopes active dry yeast
⅓ cup warm water (about 110 degrees)
1 cup sugar
2¼ cups flour
2¼ cups milk

Stir yeast into warm water in a glass measuring cup. Add a pinch of sugar and let stand at room temperature for 10 minutes, until frothy. If the yeast does not bubble, start over again with fresh yeast.

In a 5-quart or larger plastic or glass container, combine sugar and flour; whisk well. Whisk in milk and yeast mixture. Stir with a wooden or plastic spoon. Cover loosely with a kitchen towel and place on a kitchen counter overnight.

On the second day, stir, cover loosely again and refrigerate. Stir each day. On the fifth day, measure out one cup to use in baking. To remaining starter, add 1 cup flour and ½ cup sugar and stir well. Refrigerate and stir daily.

On the tenth day, measure out 1 cup to use in baking and 1 cup to give to a friend. Feed remaining starter as before with 1 cup flour and ½ cup sugar and stir.

Thereafter, feed the starter about once a week, removing two cups of the mixture at least as often.

Lou & Hy's Cheesecake

After Lou & Hy's Deli closed in 1998, its cheesecake recipe became the culinary equivalent of the holy grail. Even when the deli was in business, the cheesecake was spoken of in reverent terms. To the initiated, it inhabited a higher plane than all other cheesecakes. Akronites rejoiced when the restaurant's chef, Tage Hojfeldt, finally gave me the recipe.

The sturdy New York-style cheesecake is rich and dense, with a delicate vanilla flavor and a faint rumor of lemon. This recipe was pared down from commercial proportions, but it still makes a lot of cheesecake. Luckily, they freeze well.

Crust

4 cups graham cracker crumbs
10 tablespoons melted butter

Cake

8 (8-ounce) packages cream cheese, at room temperature
1½ cups plus 2 tablespoons flour
2¾ cups plus 2 tablespoons sugar
½ teaspoon salt
1 pint sour cream
9 eggs
2 half-pint containers whipping cream
½ cup powdered sugar
1 tablespoon vanilla extract
1 tablespoon lemon juice
Cherry, blueberry or pineapple pie filling
Whipped cream if desired

For the crust: Stir and toss crumbs with melted butter. Press equal amounts into the bottoms of four 8- or 8½-inch-round springform pans, or a 9½-, 8½- and 7½-inch pan (the sizes in most nested springform pan sets).

For the cake: In a 5-quart mixer bowl, beat cream cheese with an electric mixer until fluffy. Slowly beat in flour and then sugar. Add salt and sour cream and beat until smooth, scraping down sides occasionally with a rubber spatula.

Add eggs one at a time, beating on low speed after each addition just until egg is incorporated. Bowl will be very full. Turn off mixer. Scrape bowl and stir with a rubber spatula until batter is uniformly mixed.

In a very large bowl, beat whipping cream until slightly thickened. While beating, slowly add powdered sugar, vanilla and lemon juice until soft peaks form.

Pour one-fourth of the cream cheese mixture into the bowl with the whipped cream and fold until incorporated. Add half of remaining batter and fold again, then fold in remaining batter.

Pour over crusts in springform pans. Place in a boiling water bath and bake in a preheated, 325-degree oven for about 2½ hours; or place pans directly on oven shelves and bake in a preheated, 350-degree oven until cheesecakes are almost set. To test for doneness, gently shake pans. The cheesecakes should still wiggle slightly. Without the water bath, baking time will be about 40 minutes for a 7½-inch cake, 50 minutes for an 8- to 8½-inch cake, and 60 minutes for a 9½-inch cake.

Cool to room temperature, then refrigerate. Before serving, run a sharp knife between the cake and sides of the pan. Release the clamp, spread the sides and lift the sides off the cake. Top with pie filling and decorate with whipped cream, if desired.

Makes 3 to 4 cheesecakes, depending on pan size.

Almost Ken Stewart's White French Dressing

People are crazy about this salad dressing, which turns out to be a simple mixture of mayonnaise, grated onion, distilled white vinegar, sugar and a dab of mustard.

The trick is a heavy hand with the vinegar. You'll think it's too much, but just as your taste buds threaten to curl into a permanent pucker, an undertone of sweetness mellows everything out.

1 cup Hellman's mayonnaise

¼ cup grated yellow onion

1 teaspoon Dijon mustard

1 tablespoon plus 2 teaspoons distilled white vinegar

1 tablespoon plus 1 teaspoon sugar

Place mayonnaise in a bowl. Grate the onion on the grater disk of a food processor or the large holes of a box grater, then mince finely by hand. Measure onion, packing down. Add to mayonnaise.

Add remaining ingredients and stir well. Cover and refrigerate overnight before using.

Makes about 1 cup.

Jane Snow Cooks

Barberton Fried Chicken

....

This thick-crusted, juicy chicken is fried in lard. Don't even consider using vegetable oil—you might as well order from the Colonel.
I figured out how to make the chicken by slinking through the kitchens of Barberton's famous chicken houses and making mental notes of all I saw. The recipe is simple, but the results are glorious.

....

    2 frying chickens, cut up
    Flour
    Salt, pepper
    2 eggs, beaten
    Unseasoned, dry bread crumbs
    Lard (about 4 pounds)

Cut chicken breasts in half lengthwise; separate thighs from legs. All of the chicken pieces should be about the same size for even cooking.

Combine flour, salt and pepper. Roll chicken pieces in flour and shake off excess. Dip in beaten eggs. Roll in bread crumbs, pressing crumbs into chicken; gently shake off excess.

Melt lard in a chicken fryer or heavy, deep kettle. Heat to 350 degrees. Fry chicken pieces a few at a time for 20 minutes. Keep fried chicken warm while frying remaining batches.

Makes 4 to 6 servings.

Cannova-Style Chili

The history of this recipe is shrouded in secrecy and skullduggery. Never has a bowl of chili inspired such passion. At one point, a relative of one of the three men who claimed ownership of the recipe was choked and threatened with death if the chili was served at his Wadsworth restaurant.

I tried for years to get the recipe for the legion of fans who yearned for a bowl after Cannova's restaurant on Lakeshore Boulevard in Akron closed in 1993. Finally, I pieced it together. The brick-red chili contains plenty of fat, so it's not for everyone. It is served over spaghetti.

2 cups cubed beef suet or beef fat (in ½-inch squares)

3 pounds ground beef (coarse-ground, if available)

2 cups water

4 tablespoons pure chili powder (pure ground chilies, not a blend of spices)

1 teaspoon salt

½ teaspoon black pepper

⅛ teaspoon cayenne pepper

1 teaspoon cumin

1 teaspoon oregano

1 can (about 16 ounces) dark-red kidney beans, drained

Cooked spaghetti

Shredded longhorn cheese

Place suet in a large, heavy kettle over medium-high heat. Cover and cook, stirring occasionally, until the fat has been rendered. Remove bits of suet or solid fat with a slotted spoon and discard. You should have about 1 cup of liquid fat in kettle.

Add ground beef, cover and cook over medium-high heat until meat is no longer pink, stirring and breaking up meat occasionally.

Stir in water and chili powder, salt, black pepper, cayenne pepper, cumin and oregano. Simmer over low heat, uncovered, for about 1½ hours, until water evaporates and chili is orange and oily. Stir occasionally while chili cooks.

Warm beans in a separate pan. Add to individual portions of chili as desired. Serve in a bowl over cooked spaghetti or macaroni. Top each portion with shredded cheese.

Makes 8 to 10 servings.

Ginger Salad Dressing

Asian restaurants won't divulge the recipe for their addictive, soy sauce-based dressing, but an Akron woman claims the directions she sent are authentic. A friend begged a waiter for it, she said.

1 medium onion, coarsely chopped
½ ounce fresh ginger root, peeled
1 piece (1 inch) celery rib
½ teaspoon lemon juice
½ cup cider vinegar
1½ cups vegetable oil

½ cup soy sauce
½ medium carrot, in chunks
1 cup water
2 teaspoons ketchup
Pinch of salt, sugar, pepper
Dash of Tabasco sauce

Combine all ingredients in a blender and process until smooth. Refrigerate.

Makes 1 quart.

Herbed Roast Beef in Salt Crust

A food writer friend urged me to run this recipe. She said her readers went wild over it, and mine would, too.

She was right. Baking a roast in a crust of kosher salt mixed with water produces a juicy, brown, flavorful piece of meat that isn't a bit salty. This recipe is better than the one on the back of the Morton's Kosher Salt box. Try it and be amazed.

⅓ cup olive oil
¼ cup grated onion
1 teaspoon garlic salt
1 teaspoon dried basil
½ teaspoon dried marjoram

½ teaspoon dried thyme
¼ teaspoon pepper
1 beef rib or eye of round roast, 4 to 6 pounds
1 (3-pound) box Morton Coarse Kosher Salt
1¼ cups water

Combine oil, onion, garlic salt, basil, marjoram, thyme and pepper in a heavy plastic bag. Mix well. Add roast; coat well with marinade. Marinate in refrigerator 2 hours or overnight. (Marinating is optional; if desired, eliminate this step, along with the marinade ingredients).

Line roasting pan with foil. Combine coarse kosher salt and water to form a thick slush. Pat 1 cup of mixture into a ½-inch-thick rectangle in pan. Pat roast dry with paper towels. Insert meat thermometer. Place roast on salt layer. Sprinkle roast with a thin layer of the salt mixture, then pack remaining salt mixture around meat. Some of the salt may fall off the ends; this won't affect the final product.

Place roast in a 425-degree oven and roast 16 to 18 minutes per pound for rare (140 degrees), 20 to 22 minutes per pound for medium (160 degrees) or 25 to 30 minutes for well done (170 degrees). Remove roast when thermometer registers 5 degrees below desired doneness.

Let roast stand 5 to 10 minutes in salt crust. To remove crust, you may need to use a hammer. After removing crust, whisk away any remaining salt crystals on roast with a pastry brush.

Makes 8 to 12 servings.

Note: Use prime rib, eye of round or any beef roast that is at least 4 pounds. Smaller roasts will overcook before the crust hardens. For larger roasts, cooking time will not be much longer than for smaller roasts. Use a meat thermometer. Use only coarse kosher salt, not table salt or rock salt.

White Chili

A dynamite version served at the former Two Sisters restaurant on Main Street in Akron in the early 1990s set people talking and started my phone ringing with recipe requests. The closest I've come is a recipe provided by Ann Nauer of Akron. Her daughter won a Pennsylvania chili contest with the recipe, which produces a deeply flavored, almost creamy chili.

4 bone-in chicken breasts
3½ cups water
3 cups chicken broth
2 tablespoons olive oil
2 cups chopped onion
4 cloves minced garlic
1 (4-ounce) can chopped green chilies

2 teaspoons cumin
1 tablespoon oregano
¼ teaspoon ground cloves
¼ teaspoon cayenne pepper
Salt, pepper
2 (16-ounce) cans Great Northern beans
Shredded Monterey Jack cheese for topping

Place chicken breasts in a large pan, cover with the cold water and bring to a simmer. Simmer very gently for 20 minutes, until chicken is cooked through. Remove chicken and cool slightly, reserving liquid. Shred chicken and add to cooking liquid. Add canned chicken broth.

Heat oil in a skillet. Add onion and garlic and sauté until softened, about 10 minutes. Add chilies, cumin, oregano, cloves, cayenne and salt and pepper to taste; sauté 2 minutes. Add vegetable mixture to the pan with the chicken and broth. Add beans and simmer 1½ hours. Top each serving with Monterey Jack cheese.

Jane Snow Cooks

Sauerkraut Balls

The popularity of these deep-fried morsels of sauerkraut and ground ham never wanes in Northeast Ohio. They are on the menus of restaurants all over Akron, from the ritziest to the humblest, and were voted the city's official food by *Beacon Journal* readers in 1996. The quintessential version was served at the old Bavarian Haus, whose chef, Dick Mansfield, shared the recipe in 1995.

1¼ pounds ground ham

6 eggs

2¼ teaspoons granulated garlic
or 1 teaspoon garlic powder

1 teaspoon black pepper

¾ teaspoon cayenne pepper

1 medium onion, minced fine

5 pounds sauerkraut, drained and chopped

4 to 6 cups flour

1 egg beaten with 1 cup milk

Flour for coating

Dry, unseasoned bread crumbs

Oil for deep-frying

In a very large bowl, combine ham, eggs, garlic, peppers and onion. Add sauerkraut and mix well with your hands. Add flour a little at a time, kneading until the mixture is smooth and can be shaped into soft balls. Use only enough flour to achieve the proper consistency. The mixture will be sticky.

Pull off chunks of the mixture and roll between your palms to make balls the size of a golf ball. Place on cookie sheets and freeze until firm, about 2 hours. While frozen, roll in the flour, then in the egg-milk mixture, then in the bread crumbs. Freeze again and transfer to plastic freezer bags until ready for use, or fry immediately.

To fry, heat oil to 375 degrees. Fry a few at a time (straight from freezer) until the coating is golden brown and a fork easily pierces to the center. If the oil is too hot, the outsides will burn before the insides thaw and cook.

Makes about 96.

Kifli

Whether you call them "nut horns" or "kifli," they're the most popular cookie in Northeast Ohio, judging by the phone calls I get each December. The best recipe I've found is for the meltingly tender kifli made by members of the St. Nicholas Orthodox Church in Suffield Township for their annual bazaar.

1½ cups milk
¾ cup plus 1 tablespoon sugar
2 teaspoons salt
1 cup margarine or butter
3 eggs, beaten
½ cup warm water
3 envelopes active dry yeast
9 cups (about) unbleached flour
Nut filling (recipe follows)

Bring milk almost to a boil. Add ¾ cup sugar, salt and margarine. Cook and stir until melted, but do not boil. Cool, then beat in the eggs.

Place warm water in a medium bowl. Stir in yeast and 1 tablespoon sugar. Let stand about 2 minutes, until foamy. Stir in milk mixture.

Place flour in a large bowl. Pour yeast-milk mixture into a well in center of flour. Mix flour into liquid a little at a time until a soft dough is formed, adding flour if necessary. On a lightly floured surface, knead well until smooth.

Place dough in a large oiled bowl and turn to grease top. Cover and let rise in a warm place until doubled in bulk.

Divide into four pieces. On a floured surface, roll each piece into a square about ⅛- to ¼-inch thick. With a sharp knife, cut into 2½-inch squares. Place 1 teaspoon filling in the center of each square. Fold opposite corners over filling envelope-fashion, tucking top corner under the roll so that it will not burst open while baking.

Place on lightly greased baking sheets and let rise about 5 minutes. Bake at 350 degrees for 15 to 20 minutes. Cool on wire racks.

Nut Filling

½ cup evaporated milk

¾ cup sugar

¼ cup margarine

3 cups ground walnuts

¾ cup finely crushed vanilla wafers

¼ cup honey

½ teaspoon vanilla extract

Heat milk, sugar and margarine in a saucepan until margarine is melted. Place walnuts and wafer crumbs in a bowl; stir in milk mixture. Stir in honey and vanilla. Cool.

The Recipes

Chapter 3
Winners

A cookie that beat out 614 others in a cooking competition must be pretty awesome. And it is, as are all of the recipes in this chapter. Every one of them is a winner, either of a contest I held at the *Beacon Journal* or a contest I judged at local festival or other event.

The region has many stellar cooks who aren't afraid to put their reputations on the line. In the last two decades, I've heard from thousands of them—they sent me their best tailgating recipes, low-calorie recipes, quick-fix recipes, cheesecake recipes and once, sadly, their fruitcake recipes.

An avowed fruitcake hater, I dared fruitcake lovers to change my mind by dropping off a fruitcake and the recipe at the newspaper. I figured I'd get ten or so, but they began arriving in droves. The dreaded cakes formed drifts around my desk. We had to commandeer mail carts to transport them in batches from the lobby. The irony was not lost on us when I and a couple of other fruitcake haters had to sample fruitcakes steadily for about four hours to choose a winner. Even fruitcake haters may like the recipe for applesauce fruitcake in this chapter.

Other contests, such as Best Cook in the Office, were much more fun. When I asked people to nominate a co-worker for the title, the faxes poured in from hospitals, factories, rectories and city halls across the region. The best office party dish, whose recipe was a secret until we coaxed it out of the cook, was a yummy Mexican appetizer cheesecake that's served with tortilla chips for dipping.

I regularly make the luscious chicken lasagna that won a Mother's Day contest, and the artichoke-pine nut pasta chosen by three University of Akron chefs as the winner of a Five Easy Pieces contest for quick recipes of five ingredients or less. In fact, most of the recipes in this chapter have found a spot in my personal recipe file. They're all winners.

Fettuccine with Four Cheeses

Easy holiday entertaining was the theme and a rich pasta and mushroom casserole was the winner of a 1986 search for party dishes that could be made in less than an hour. Christine Gaino of Copley combined fettuccine with mushrooms in a nutmeg-scented cream sauce enriched with mozzarella, Fontina, Gruyére and Parmesan cheeses.

½ pound thinly sliced prosciutto

1 pound fresh mushrooms

7 large, canned Italian plum tomatoes (about half of a 28-ounce can)

12 tablespoons butter

1 cup beef broth

2 large onions, chopped

4 tablespoons flour

2 cups milk

2 cups half and half

Salt, white pepper, dash of nutmeg

1 tablespoon olive oil

1½ pounds fettuccine

2 tablespoons melted butter

½ cup each grated mozzarella, Fontina, Gruyére and Parmesan cheeses

Chop prosciutto. Thinly slice fresh mushrooms. Drain tomatoes, discarding liquid; finely dice tomatoes. Heat 4 tablespoons butter in deep skillet. Sauté prosciutto and fresh mushrooms for 5 minutes; add tomatoes and beef broth. Boil over high heat until liquid evaporates and mixture is thick. Set aside.

Heat 8 tablespoons butter in deep kettle. Sauté onions for 5 minutes. Purée onions in blender or food processor. Return to kettle and add flour. Stir for a minute, then add milk and half-and-half, whisking until smooth. Add salt, pepper and nutmeg and cook and stir until mixture comes to a boil. Remove from heat. Sauce will be thin.

Cook pasta in boiling water with olive oil until al dente, about 10 minutes. Drain and toss with melted butter. In a medium bowl, combine cheeses. To assemble, spread a thin coating of white sauce on bottom of 9-by-12-by-2-inch lasagna pan. Spread half the noodles over sauce. Dab half of the prosciutto-mushroom mixture over noodles. Ladle about half the remaining white sauce over noodles. Top with half the grated cheeses. Repeat layering, ending with cheeses.

Bake at 350 degrees for about 40 to 50 minutes, or until top is brown and bubbly.

Makes 12 servings.

Green Tomato Chicken with Oregano

This unusual dish was a finalist in the newspaper's Great Tomato Contest in August 1985. Although it didn't earn top prize for Patricia Coons, there's no doubt the recipe is a winner. We didn't know green tomatoes could taste so good.

2 to 2½ pounds frying chicken, cut in pieces, or 6 chicken breast halves
Flour
3 tablespoons vegetable oil
6 medium green tomatoes
4 medium onions, peeled
1 apple, peeled, seeded and sliced
1 tablespoon oregano
2 teaspoons sugar
½ teaspoon each nutmeg, salt
1 cup heavy cream
Buttered toast points

Skin chicken. Dredge in flour and shake off excess. Brown on all sides in oil, then cover pan and steam 20 minutes over medium-low heat. Cut meat into 1-inch cubes, discarding bones.

Slice tomatoes and onions into quarter-inch wedges and sauté for 7 to 8 minutes in chicken pan. Stir in apple, oregano, sugar, nutmeg, salt and chicken cubes and simmer for 5 minutes. Add cream and simmer over medium heat until thick. Serve hot over toast points.

Makes 6 servings.

Mexican Cheesecake Appetizer

Yes, it's a cheesecake. No, it isn't dessert. Diane Zgonc's creamy, spicy cheesecake studded with bits of chicken won the newspaper's Best Cook in the Office contest in 1997. Place it on a buffet with a knife to cut it into slivers or with sturdy chips for dipping. You'll never go back to cheese balls.

2 teaspoons chicken bouillon granules

½ cup hot water

3 (8-ounce) packages cream cheese, softened

1½ teaspoons chili powder

½ to 1 teaspoon hot pepper sauce

2 eggs

1 cup finely chopped cooked chicken

1 tablespoon (or less) minced jalapeño peppers

1 pint sour cream

½ cup salsa

1 cup shredded Cheddar cheese

Chopped green onions

Tortilla chips

Dissolve bouillon in hot water and set aside. Beat cream cheese with chili powder and pepper sauce until smooth. Add eggs and mix well. Add bouillon mixture and beat until smooth. Stir in chicken and jalapeños.

Pour into a lightly greased, 9-inch springform pan. Bake at 325 degrees for 35 minutes, or until set around the edges but still slightly jiggly in the center. Cool 15 minutes in pan. Run a knife around edge of pan and remove sides. Before serving, mix sour cream and salsa. Spread over cheesecake. Sprinkle with Cheddar cheese and onions. Surround with tortilla chips. Serve warm or chilled.

Savage Beast Cheesecake

The winner of the *Beacon Journal* Low-Cal Cooking Contest in 1988 was a cloud-like cheesecake studded with strawberries, topped with a meringue pouf and drizzled with more berries and juice.

Carol Liederbach of Sagamore Hills made up the recipe after going on a diet. "Nothing soothes the savage beast more than a big, sweet, fluffy dessert," she wrote.

5 egg whites

2 packets (1 gram each) Sweet 'n Low

2 cups diced strawberries, fresh or frozen

1 envelope unflavored gelatin

½ cup water

2 cups skim milk

8 ounces Neufchatel cheese, softened

1 (1.1-ounce) small box low-calorie, instant vanilla pudding mix

1 teaspoon vanilla extract

Place 2 of the egg whites in a deep bowl and bring to room temperature. With an electric mixer, beat until fluffy. Add 1 packet Sweet 'n Low and continue beating until stiff peaks form. Place baking parchment paper on a cookie sheet. With a spoon, drop egg whites onto the paper into eight high, rounded mounds. Bake at 250 degrees for about 40 minutes, until brown. Turn off oven and let meringues cool in oven.

If using fresh strawberries, combine with ¼ cup of the water and set aside. If using frozen berries, dice and set aside with some of the juice. Sprinkle gelatin over remaining ¼ cup of the water in a measuring cup. Place cup in a small pan of warm water until gelatin is dissolved.

Combine milk and cheese in a blender or food processor and process until smooth. Slowly add gelatin mixture, dry pudding mix and vanilla and process until combined. Whip remaining 3 egg whites until fluffy.

Sprinkle 1 packet of Sweet 'n Low over egg whites and continue beating until stiff but not dry. Fold cheese mixture and 1½ cups drained, diced strawberries into the egg whites.

Divide into eight large, fancy dessert dishes and chill. If a round, firm cheesecake is desired, reduce the skim milk to 1½ cups and pour the cheesecake mixture into an 8-inch springform pan sprayed with vegetable oil. Chill.

To serve, place a meringue pouf on each serving and top with remaining berries and juice.

Makes 8 servings.

Calories per serving: 186. Protein: 12 grams. Fat: 7 grams. Cholesterol: 19 grams. Sodium: 259 milligrams.

Green Beans Supreme

This fresh take on the standard green-bean casserole eschews canned soup in favor of a lemon-spiked sour cream sauce. The recipe was a winner for Betty Hinton of Akron in the *Beacon Journal*'s 1983 Great Vegetable Cookoff.

5 cups fresh green beans, in 1-inch pieces

1 tablespoon plus 1 teaspoon salt

1 medium onion, sliced and separated into rings

1 tablespoon minced fresh parsley

2 tablespoons butter or margarine

1 tablespoon flour

¼ teaspoon pepper

1 teaspoon grated lemon peel

1 cup sour cream

½ cup shredded Cheddar cheese

2 tablespoons melted butter or margarine

½ cup dry bread crumbs

Place green beans and a tablespoon of salt in a very large kettle filled with boiling water. Boil, stirring occasionally, for 4 to 8 minutes, or just until beans are tender-crisp. Drain in colander and immediately plunge beans into ice water. Drain and set aside.

Sauté onion and parsley in butter until tender but not brown, about 10 minutes. Remove from heat and add flour, 1 teaspoon salt, pepper and lemon peel. Add sour cream and mix well. Return to heat and stir in beans. When beans are hot, turn into a buttered 10-by-6-inch baking dish. Sprinkle with shredded cheese. Combine melted butter and bread crumbs and sprinkle over cheese. Broil until cheese melts and crumbs are brown.

Makes 6 servings.

Velvet Corn Soup

The delicate chowder 'looks like an impressionist painting,' according to judges of the *Beacon Journal*'s Kettle of Soup contest in 1989. The recipe earned top prize for Bob White of Cuyahoga Falls.

6 cups chicken broth

¼ pound medium shrimp, peeled, deveined and chopped coarse

½ cup diced, cooked ham

¼ cup coarse-chopped water chestnuts

1 (16¾-ounce) can cream-style corn

2 teaspoons sesame oil

½ teaspoon salt

⅛ teaspoon white pepper

3 tablespoons cornstarch mixed with ⅓ cup water

2 egg whites, lightly beaten

1 green onion (including top), sliced thin

Bring broth to a boil in a 3-quart pot. Add shrimp, ham, water chestnuts, corn, sesame oil, salt and pepper. Return to a simmer.

Add cornstarch mixture and cook, stirring, until soup boils and thickens slightly. Remove from heat and slowly drizzle in egg whites, stirring constantly. Sprinkle green onion on each serving.

Makes 6 to 8 servings.

Applesauce Fruitcake

A panel of fruitcake haters chose this crunchy, relatively airy cake as tops among 158 entries in the *Beacon Journal's* I Hate Fruitcake Contest. Coconut gives it a lovely flavor.

½ pound candied red cherries
½ pound candied green cherries
½ pound candied pineapple
½ pound dates (optional)
2½ cups flour
¾ cup shortening
2 cups sugar
3 eggs

½ teaspoon salt
½ tablespoon vanilla extract
1 cup applesauce
1½ teaspoons baking soda
½ pound flaked coconut
½ pound pecans
½ pound walnuts

Chop fruits into half-inch pieces. With hands, toss fruit with ½ cup flour, coating each piece well.

Cream together shortening and sugar. Beat in eggs one at a time. Stir in salt, vanilla, applesauce and soda. Gradually add remaining flour. Stir in chopped fruits, coconut, pecans and walnuts.

Line bottoms and sides of 2 loaf pans with two layers of waxed paper.

Fill pans three-fourths full and bake at 375 degrees for 30 minutes. Reduce heat to 275 degrees and bake 1½ to 2 hours longer. Let cakes stand in pans for 5 minutes at room temperature. Remove from pans and peel off waxed paper. When cakes are cool, wrap in plastic wrap and store in a cool place.

Jane Snow Cooks

Tomato & Corn Bisque

A hearty but sophisticated tomato-corn bisque won top prize for Deborah Norin in the *Beacon Journal's* Tailgate Picnic Contest. The soup is chunky with bits of tomato, corn and green pepper. Melted Monterey Jack cheese gives it a rich, smooth texture.

5 tablespoons unsalted butter	1 tablespoon tomato paste
1 cup chopped onions	1 teaspoon chili powder
1 teaspoon chopped garlic	¾ teaspoon salt
¼ cup chopped green pepper	1½ cups grated Monterey Jack cheese
1½ cups corn kernels (about 3 ears)	1 cup sour cream
4 large tomatoes, stemmed and quartered	12 slices bacon, fried crisp and crumbled
4 cups chicken broth	

Melt butter in a large, heavy pot. Sauté onions, garlic and green pepper until softened. Add corn and tomatoes and cook, stirring, for 3 minutes.

Add chicken broth, tomato paste, chili powder and salt. Stir. Bring to a boil, reduce heat and simmer until vegetables are tender, about 25 minutes.

Purée soup in a blender or food processor. Cool; cover and chill. Before serving, reheat soup over low heat. Add cheese, one-fourth cup at a time, allowing it to melt before next addition. To serve, pour soup into mugs and top each serving with a dollop of sour cream and a sprinkling of bacon bits.

Strawberry Potato Chocolate Cake

Portage County's village of Mantua used to supply most of the potatoes for Ohio's potato chip industry. Most of the potato farmers are gone, but great potato recipes still abound at the annual potato festival. This fancy chocolate cake earned first prize for Selma King of Hudson in the 2006 contest.

1 cup plain mashed potatoes	2 cups sugar
⅔ cup water	4 eggs
¼ teaspoon salt	2 (1-ounce) squares unsweetened chocolate, melted
1 tablespoon butter	
2 cups flour	1 teaspoon vanilla extract
1 teaspoon baking soda	1 quart strawberries, sliced
1 teaspoon salt	1½ cups (about) strawberry pie gel (purchased is fine)
1 cup (2 sticks) butter, softened	

Mash potatoes again until smooth, adding in the water, salt and 1 tablespoon butter. Set aside. Sift together flour, soda and 1 teaspoon salt.

Preheat oven to 375 degrees. Grease and flour two 8-inch round baking pans. In a mixer bowl, cream together softened butter and sugar until fluffy. Add eggs one at a time, beating thoroughly after each addition. Add melted chocolate and vanilla. Alternately add potatoes and flour mixture, mixing well after each addition.

Pour batter equally into pans. Bake at 375 degrees for 35 minutes, until toothpick inserted in the center comes out clean. Let cool 10 minutes in pans, then remove from pans and cool completely on a wire rack.

Place one layer onto serving plate, then cut a 3-inch wide hole in the center of it. Save the crumbs. Fill hole with strawberries and glaze and cover the rim of the cake with strawberry slices and glaze. Carefully place the second cake layer on top. Frost cake with your favorite white icing. Crumble the cake crumbs on the top and decorate with strawberries.

Lemon-Lavender Blueberry Scones

Luscious Lemon-Lavender Blueberry Scones were voted tops at the first Lavender Festival at DayBreak Farm in Streetsboro in 2006, where I was on hand to taste and judge. The winner was Monica Wagner of Moreland Hills.

2 cups all-purpose flour

1 cup whole-wheat flour

1 tablespoon baking powder

½ teaspoon baking soda

½ teaspoon salt

8 tablespoons cold, unsalted butter

1 tablespoon dried lavender blossoms

Grated zest (outer yellow skin) of 1 lemon

1 tablespoon fresh lemon juice

⅔ cup buttermilk

½ cup sugar

1 egg

1 cup fresh blueberries

Blend dry ingredients in a large mixing bowl. Cut in butter with a pastry blender or two forks until the mixture resembles bread crumbs. Sprinkle lavender over the mixture.

In another bowl mix lemon zest, lemon juice, buttermilk, sugar and egg. Pour over dry ingredients. Stir with a fork until a soft dough forms. Add blueberries and mix briefly with hands just until dough clings together. Turn onto a floured surface.

Form dough into 2 balls, then flatten with hands into circles, each about ½ inch thick. Cut each circle into 8 wedges. Bake on parchment-lined baking sheets at 375 degrees for 20 to 25 minutes, until light golden brown.

Makes 16 scones.

Happy Birthday Pine Nut Pasta

A suave toss of penne pasta, artichoke hearts, pine nuts, feta cheese and sun-dried tomatoes beat 734 other recipes in the *Beacon Journal*'s Five Easy Pieces recipe contest. Marie-France Londa of Fairlawn created the 20-minute pasta recipe after having a similar dish on her birthday in a fancy restaurant.

  2 cups dry penne pasta
  1 (3-ounce) package sun-dried tomatoes
  ⅓ cup pine nuts
  1 (6-ounce) jar marinated artichoke hearts
  1 cup crumbled feta cheese

Cook pasta in boiling water until al dente. Meanwhile, pour boiling water over tomatoes and let stand 8 to 10 minutes to soften. Toast pine nuts in a dry skillet over medium-high heat, shaking occasionally, until lightly browned.

Chop artichoke hearts into quarters, reserving marinade. Chop softened tomatoes.

Drain pasta. Place feta cheese in a large, deep skillet and stir over medium heat. When cheese begins to melt, add pasta and continue stirring to coat noodles. Stir in remaining ingredients, including the marinade from the artichokes.

Makes 4 servings.

Jane Snow Cooks

Mocha Viennese Shortbread

Mocha Viennese Shortbread Cookies are a tapestry of flavors and textures—meltingly rich shortbread fingers, a creamy, coffee-chocolate filling, and glossy, brittle chocolate-dipped tips. The sophisticated cookie recipe from Laura Carbone of Kent won the 1994 *Beacon Journal* Christmas Cookie Contest.

1 cup plus 2 tablespoons unsalted butter, softened

½ cup sifted confectioners' sugar

½ teaspoon vanilla extract

2 cups all-purpose flour (unsifted)

¼ teaspoon baking powder

⅔ cup unsifted confectioners' sugar

1 teaspoon instant coffee dissolved in 1 teaspoon water

6 ounces coating chocolate (available in cake-supply shops) or semisweet chocolate chips

In a medium bowl, cream 1 cup of the butter with the ½ cup sifted confectioners' sugar and the vanilla until fluffy. In another bowl, stir together the flour and baking powder with a whisk until thoroughly mixed. Stir the flour mixture into the creamed mixture.

Using a cookie press and a medium star No. 32 tip (or a pastry bag with a star tip, or a plastic bag with one tiny bit of a corner snipped off), make dough strips 3 inches long on an ungreased baking sheet. Place strips 1 inch apart. Bake at 350 degrees for about 7 minutes, or until very lightly browned around the edges. Cool.

Meanwhile, mix remaining 2 tablespoons butter with the ⅔ cup unsifted confectioners' sugar and the instant coffee mixture. Beat until creamy. When cookies are cool, spread a small amount on the flat side of one cookie and cover with the flat side of another cookie, making a sandwich. Repeat until all cookies are used.

Melt coating chocolate or chocolate chips. Dip about one-half inch of both ends of each cookie in the chocolate, and place on a tray lined with waxed paper. Chill until chocolate is firm. Store in a tightly sealed container.

Makes about 2 dozen cookies.

Chicken Lasagna

When I asked readers to send me essays about the best dish their mothers cook, I got a smorgasbord of memories, along with this winning recipe from Diana Duque of Munroe Falls.

4 bone-in chicken breast halves	2 cups ketchup
4 boneless pork chops (about ½ pound)	⅓ cup tomato paste
1¾ cups water	½ cup whipping cream
1 clove garlic, minced	½ teaspoon grated nutmeg
½ teaspoon Italian seasoning	3 cups shredded mozzarella
Salt, pepper	2 cups grated Parmesan
1 chicken bouillon cube	3 tablespoons snipped parsley
¼ pound bacon	12 lasagna noodles, cooked and drained
1 large onion, chopped fine	1 tablespoon butter, cut in small pieces

Place chicken breasts and pork in water. Add garlic, Italian seasoning, salt, pepper and bouillon cube. Cover and simmer gently until meat is tender, about 45 minutes. Remove and cool meat; Measure out and return to pan 2 cups of broth, discarding rest.

Cook bacon in a skillet until crisp. Remove and drain. In bacon grease, sauté onion until tender. Add onion to meat broth along with ketchup and tomato paste. Simmer uncovered over medium heat for about 1 hour, stirring frequently, until thick. Cool to room temperature. Stir in cream and nutmeg.

Shred cooked chicken and pork, discarding chicken skin and bones. Crumble bacon. Combine all three in a bowl. In another bowl, combine cheeses and parsley.

Spread 1 cup of the sauce in a 9-by-13½-inch baking dish. Arrange 3 lasagna noodles over sauce. Spread more sauce over noodles. Sprinkle with half of the meat and one-third of the cheese. Repeat. Top with another layer of lasagna noodles and remaining cheese. Dot with butter.

Bake at 350 degrees, about 45 minutes, until hot and bubbly. Let stand 10 minutes before cutting.

Makes 8 servings.

Choco-Orange Brownies

The winner of a brownie contest I judged in 1990 at the Zona Spray Cooking School in Hudson was this chocolate-orange bar from Christine King of Hiram. The inspiration was the chocolate-orange candy a family in her hometown made when she was a child.

¾ cup unsalted butter	1 tablespoon grated orange rind
4 ounces unsweetened chocolate	1⅔ cups flour
2 cups sugar	1 teaspoon baking powder
4 eggs at room temperature	1 teaspoon salt
1 teaspoon orange extract	Confectioners' sugar
1 teaspoon vanilla extract	Peel of 1 orange

In medium saucepan over low heat, melt butter until it begins to soften. Add chocolate and continue to melt, whisking until smooth. Stir in sugar and remove from heat. With wire whisk, beat in eggs one at a time. Stir in extracts and orange rind.

Mix flour, baking powder and salt together in a small bowl. Add to chocolate mixture and stir until blended. Spread in a lightly greased, glass 9-by-13-inch baking pan. Bake at 350 degrees for 35 minutes or until top has a dull crust and a slight imprint remains when touched. Cool completely. With a sifter, dust with confectioners' sugar.

With a vegetable peeler, remove the thin orange part of the peel in about 1-inch strips. Cut the strips into thin slivers with a paring knife. Plunge into boiling water for 30 seconds to soften. Drain and dry on paper towels.

Cut brownies into big squares. Arrange slivers of orange peel on each brownie in a star-burst pattern.

Tomato Oatmeal Soup

A luscious, garlic-scented soup from Mazatlan earned Margaret Snyder of Norton top prize in the *Beacon Journal*'s Great Tomato Contest. The toasted oatmeal that thickens the soup gives it a nutty flavor.

1 cup dry oatmeal
1 stick butter
1 medium onion, chopped
3 cloves garlic, crushed
2 large ripe tomatoes, peeled, seeded and chopped
2 quarts chicken broth
Salt, pepper

Sprinkle oatmeal in an ungreased skillet and brown carefully over low heat, stirring constantly, for about 10 minutes. In a large saucepan, melt butter and sauté onion and garlic until onion is almost transparent and barely tender. Stir in chopped tomato and chicken broth. Add browned oatmeal and simmer, uncovered for 6 minutes. Season with salt and pepper to taste.

Almond Crèmes

These small sandwich cookies are so flaky they crumble in your mouth. The almond-flavored filling is a creamy counterpoint. The cookies beat out 614 others to take top prize for Betty Hilton of Mogadore in the 2002 *Beacon Journal* Holiday Cookie Contest.

1 cup flour	¾ cup sifted confectioners' sugar
6 tablespoons chilled butter	1 tablespoon softened butter
3½ tablespoons half and half, divided	⅛ teaspoon almond extract
Powdered sugar for dipping	

Place flour in a medium bowl. Cut chilled butter into small pieces and cut into flour with a pastry blender until crumbs are the size of small peas.

Reserve 1 tablespoon of the half and half for use in the filling. Sprinkle 1 of the remaining tablespoons over part of the flour mixture and toss with a fork to moisten. Sprinkle another tablespoon over more of the flour mixture and toss with a fork. Sprinkle last half-tablespoon over flour mixture and toss to moisten.

Gather dough into a ball. Do not knead or handle more than necessary. Divide dough in half. Roll out on a floured board to slightly less than ⅛-inch thick. Cut into 1½-inch squares.

Dip one side of each dough square in powdered sugar. Place sugared side up, a half-inch apart, on ungreased baking sheets. With a fork, prick each cookie in parallel rows. Bake at 375 degrees for 8 minutes, or until golden and puffy. Cool on wire racks.

While pastry cools, make the filling by combining confectioners' sugar, softened butter, almond extract and reserved 1 tablespoon half and half. Beat until smooth, adding more liquid or sugar if necessary to achieve a thick spreading consistency.

When the cookies are cool, sandwich in pairs with the almond filling. Store at room temperature, loosely covered.

Makes 2½ dozen.

The Recipes

Chapter 4
Jane's Favorites

With the thousands of recipes that cross my desk each year, a recipe has to be very special to make it into my personal file. OK, "file" is overstating it. I toss the recipes I want to keep into a big cream-and-blue mixing bowl on my kitchen shelf. In three decades, I've tossed in just 30 or 40 recipes. I'm sharing the best of them in this chapter.

A couple of the recipes are from readers, one is from a chef and one is from a caterer. The rest are mine.

In the mid-1980s, I began creating the recipes that ran with my newspaper articles, initially because most recipes in cookbooks and press releases were too long and complicated for working women and men to tackle on week nights. Cookbooks had not kept pace with our evolving society.

Later, I continued to create recipes in order to respond quickly to trends and also because I liked the challenge of coming up with great-tasting recipes with the least amount of work. The recipes for Chicken Mole and Pad Thai in this chapter are examples of complex dishes that have been streamlined without, I think, any sacrifice in flavor.

My refrigerator was strange territory, though. It might be filled with four cheesecakes one week and a couple of gallons of homemade café mocha the next. Once I built a charcoal fire, placed two chickens on my lone grill, and drove the other two chickens to a friend's house to cook on his grill. All this before 10 A.M.

Because I was continually creating recipes, I rarely cooked the same thing twice. The recipes in the cream-and-blue mixing bowl are the exceptions. They reflect my love of big, bold flavors and my adventurous palate. Szechuan Ribs with Hot Chili Oil have both qualities, and were an adventure to make, too. The power went out, plunging my kitchen into darkness the evening I was creating the recipe.

I gathered up ribs, marinade and sauce and drove to a friend's home in Cuyahoga Falls, where the electricity was still flowing. I mixed, marinated, grilled and then we ate. My friend urged me to use his kitchen anytime. You'll know why when you taste those ribs.

Choco-Caramel Brownies

The ultimate chocolate brownie is moist and fudgy but not chewy. It's incredibly chocolatey, and it tastes like a million bucks. The brownie recipe was shared by chocolate mail-order maven Elaine "Madame Chocolate" Sherman at a Chicago food conference many years ago, and has been my favorite go-to brownie recipe ever since.

8oz. block caramel (available in candy supply stores)

1 cup plus 2 tablespoons unsalted butter, room temperature

¼ cup cream

1 teaspoon vanilla extract

12 ounces good-quality semi-sweet chocolate, melted and warm

1⅓ cups sugar

6 eggs

1 cup cake flour

Powdered sugar

Line a 9-by-13-inch baking pan with parchment or waxed paper. Butter and flour entire pan.

In a heavy saucepan over low heat, stir together caramel, 2 tablespoons butter, cream and vanilla until mixture is melted and smooth. Set aside. Chop chocolate into small pieces and place in double boiler over hot water. Stir until smooth.

Pour chocolate into a mixing bowl. Beat 1 cup butter into warm chocolate. Beat in sugar. Add eggs one at a time, beating until mixture lightens. Blend in flour just until it disappears. Pour into pan. Slowly pour caramel mixture over chocolate batter, so that it spreads evenly.

Bake at 350 degrees for 35 minutes or until a toothpick inserted 1 inch from edge has a dry crumb. Cool in pan. Dust with powdered sugar and cut into squares.

Jane Snow Cooks

Chicken Tarragon in Puff Pastry

When you want an elegant but quick meal, here's your go-to recipe. Gorgeous pastry-wrapped bundles of chicken are filled with herbed soft cheese that oozes out with the first cut of a knife. Switch the cream cheese for goat cheese or Brie for a more sophisticated flavor.

1 sheet (half of a 17½-ounce box) frozen puff pastry

3 ounces cream cheese

1 teaspoon dried tarragon

2 boneless, skinless chicken breast halves

1 egg, beaten with a fork

Thaw the pastry sheet at room temperature for 20 to 30 minutes, until pliable. Unfold sheet on a lightly floured surface. With a rolling pin, roll to a 10-by-12-inch rectangle.

With a sharp knife, cut the rectangle in half lengthwise, then cut each half into a 6-inch square with some pastry left over. Set aside the squares. With a knife tip or a chopstick, draw 1½-inch hearts on 2 scraps of pastry. Cut out the hearts with a knife. Set aside.

Mash together the cream cheese and tarragon until thoroughly combined. Place chicken breasts, smooth side down, on a work surface and pound with a blunt object (a wooden mallet or the side of a pan) until the thickness is even.

Scoop half of the cream cheese mixture into the center of each chicken breast. Draw the chicken around the cheese in the shape of a ball, sealing in cheese. Holding the seams together with your hands, place seam-side down in the center of a pastry square. Brush edges of pastry square with some of the egg. Gather pastry around the chicken, pinching pastry seams together and forming rounded bundles. Repeat with remaining chicken breast.

Place seam sides down on a lightly greased baking sheet. Brush pastry bundles with egg. Brush one side of each heart with egg, and place egg-side down in center of each pastry bundle. Brush top of heart with egg. Bake at 400 degrees for 25 minutes.

Makes 2 servings.

Chicken Mole

Chicken mole (pronounced moh-LAY) is a classic Mexican dish from the state of Oaxaca. The sauce is made with ground nuts, raisins, chili peppers and bitter chocolate. When combined with spices such as cinnamon and coriander, they weave a rich tapestry of flavors. This is my streamlined food-processor version of the usually time-intensive dish. Serve the chicken and sauce over rice, accompanied by warm flour tortillas.

2 dried poblano or ancho chili peppers

2 medium-sized ripe tomatoes, seeded and chopped

1 small onion, quartered

2 cloves garlic, halved

2 tablespoons sesame seeds

½ cup almonds

¼ cup raisins

¼ teaspoon ground cloves

¼ teaspoon cinnamon

¼ teaspoon ground coriander

1 tablespoon water

6 tablespoons vegetable oil

2 cups chicken broth

1 ounce unsweetened chocolate or ¼ cup chocolate chips

2 frying chickens, cut into pieces

Salt, pepper

Remove stems and seeds from chili peppers and tear into pieces. Place in a food processor or blender. Add tomatoes, onion, garlic, sesame seeds, almonds, raisins, cloves, cinnamon, coriander and water. Purée until mixture is smooth.

Heat 2 tablespoons of the oil in a small saucepan. Add puréed mixture and cook over low heat, stirring often, for 10 minutes. Add 1 cup of the chicken broth and chocolate. Cook over low heat, stirring often, for 10 minutes longer. Remove from heat and set aside.

Wash chicken pieces and pat dry. Sprinkle all over with salt and pepper. Heat remaining 4 tablespoons of oil in a large, deep kettle. Brown chicken pieces in batches on all sides. Return all chicken pieces to pot. Pour sauce over chicken. Add remaining 1 cup chicken broth. Cover and simmer for 45 minutes, or until chicken is very tender.

Makes 8 servings.

Jane Snow Cooks

Hot Buttered Rum

Standard hot buttered rum is kind of a blah drink that tastes mostly of liquor and water, with a scum of melted butter floating on the top. Mine, though, is caramel-y and rich, with layers of buttery flavor. The butter mixture can be made in batches and stored for weeks in the refrigerator.

1 stick (8 tablespoons) butter, softened

6 tablespoons packed brown sugar

¼ cup molasses or dark corn syrup

Rum

Boiling water

Whipped cream

With the back of a spoon, mash together butter, brown sugar and molasses in a small bowl until thoroughly mixed. Place 1 or 2 rounded teaspoons of mixture (or to taste) in a mug. Add 1 ounce of rum. Fill with boiling water, stirring until butter mixture has melted. Top with whipped cream.

Makes enough butter mixture for about 12 drinks.

Garlic Pork in Lettuce Leaves

This recipe began life as Korean-Style Steak and Lettuce Wraps from *Eating Well's Healthy in a Hurry* cookbook. But I had pork in the fridge, not steak, and I didn't like the way the meat was seasoned, and I couldn't find the cilantro I thought was in the crisper. So let's just call this a brand-new recipe. It has become one of my favorite healthful, quick-fix meals

¾ pound boneless, thin-sliced pork chops or pork tenderloin

4 tablespoons soy sauce

2 cloves minced garlic

¼ cup lemon juice

1 cup cucumber batons about ¼-inch wide and 3 inches long

3 green onions, sliced (including green part)

12 grape tomatoes, halved

½ cup fresh mint leaves

½ cup fresh basil leaves

1 teaspoon sugar

½ teaspoon crushed red pepper flakes

2 tablespoons oil

1 head leaf lettuce, leaves separated

Cut pork into ½-inch-wide strips. Place in a zipper-lock bag with half of the soy, half of the garlic and half of the lemon juice. Seal and squeeze to mix well. Refrigerate for 30 to 60 minutes.

Mound cucumber, sliced onions, tomato, mint and basil in separate piles on a platter. In a small bowl, combine sugar and red pepper flakes with remaining soy sauce, garlic and lemon juice; mix well.

Heat a large skillet over high heat. When the heat shimmers, add the oil. When the oil is hot, drain the meat, discarding the liquid. Stir-fry meat in the oil just until no longer pink. Remove from pan with a slotted spoon and mound on the platter.

At the table, wrap some of the pork and other ingredients in a lettuce leaf, sprinkling with the soy mixture before enclosing the filling. Eat with your hands.

Makes 2 to 3 servings.

Champagne Sangria

Champagne sangria is a festive drink to serve at a party. It's a colorful, big drink that is low enough in alcohol content that partygoers can glug a couple without getting tipsy. Use an inexpensive sparkling wine, not the good stuff, because all you'll taste are fruit and bubbles.

3 (12-ounce) cans Knudson Light Mango Spritzer

1 cup mango nectar

1 large orange, cut into ½-inch cubes (with skin)

2 limes, cut into ½-inch cubes (with skin)

1 large lemon, cut into ½-inch cubes (with skin)

1 cup seedless grapes, halved

1 to 2 ripe pears, cored and cut into ½-inch cubes

2 tablespoons powdered sugar

2 bottles inexpensive sparkling wine

Early in the day, pour spritzers and mango nectar into a half-gallon pitcher. Add enough of the fruit to fill the pitcher. Stir in powdered sugar. Refrigerate.

To serve, ladle some of the fruit into a wine goblet and fill halfway with the mango macerating liquid. Fill rest of way with sparkling wine.

Makes at least 12 drinks.

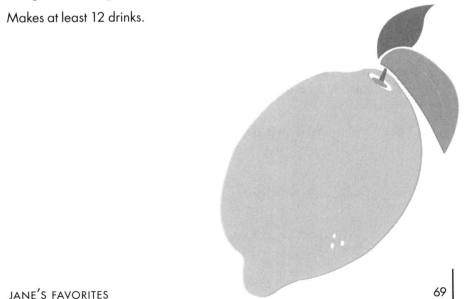

Pad Thai

Many recipes for this Thai peanut-noodle dish are too complicated for week-night cooking. Not this streamlined version, which has all the flavor for half the work.

½ pound rice noodles, ⅛-inch wide

Warm water

½ pound boneless pork, trimmed of fat

1 tablespoon nam pla (fish sauce)

¼ cup plus 2 tablespoons sugar

¼ cup plus 2 tablespoons white wine vinegar

1 tablespoon ketchup

1 tablespoon hoisin sauce

1 tablespoon peanut butter

½ cup oil

2 cloves garlic, minced

4 green onions, sliced

2 eggs, beaten

¾ cup ground roasted peanuts

2 tablespoons ground, dried red chilies

Soak noodles for 20 minutes in warm water to cover. They should be flexible but not mushy. Drain well.

Meanwhile, cut pork (boneless chops are a good cut to use) in pieces and pulse off and on in food processor until coarsely ground. Make sauce by combining nam pla, sugar, vinegar, ketchup, hoisin sauce and peanut butter, and mixing well. Heat oil in a large, heavy skillet. Add garlic and stir-fry briefly. Add pork and stir-fry until no longer pink, breaking into fine pieces. Add drained noodles and onions and toss lightly to coat with oil.

Add the sauce and bring to a rapid boil, gently folding the noodles until they absorb all of the sauce. Push the noodles to one side of the skillet.

Pour in half the beaten eggs and cover with the noodles. Repeat on other side. Cook until eggs are set. Add peanuts and fold the eggs and peanuts into the noodles.

Place noodles on a large platter. Garnish with chopped chilies.

Fresh Tomato-Ciabatta Pizza

I make this easy, fresh-flavored pizza often in the summer, adding a handful of chopped fresh basil and a pinch of sea salt to the tomato-garlic mixture. The recipe, from Noreen Stone of Hinckley Township, was a runner-up in the *Beacon Journal*'s Five Easy Pieces contest.

1 loaf ciabatta bread
3 tablespoons olive oil
4 to 8 cloves garlic, chopped
2 large tomatoes, chopped
1 cup grated mozzarella cheese

Cut loaf of bread in half lengthwise. Place on cookie sheet, cut sides up.

In a bowl, combine oil, garlic and tomatoes. Spoon onto ciabatta bread. Top with cheese. Bake at 375 degrees for 15 to 20 minutes.

Makes 4 servings.

Cantaloupe Sorbet

When you spoon up chef Zachary Bruell's sorbets, you'd swear you were sitting under a tree eating a wonderful new kind of fruit—a kind that turns to creamy slush when you bite into it.

1 medium cantaloupe
1 cup plus 2 tablespoons sugar

Cut the cantaloupe in fourths and scrape out the seeds. Cut each piece in half lengthwise again and pare off the rind. Cut into chunks and purée in two batches in the bowl of a food processor. You should have about 2½ cups purée. Transfer to a bowl, add sugar and stir until blended.

Pour into the canister of an ice cream maker and churn until the consistency of soft-serve frozen yogurt (about 40 minutes in a bucket-style churn). Spoon into lidded plastic containers and freeze at least 2 hours, or until firm.

Makes about 3 cups.

Note: The Cleveland chef's formula of 2½ cups purée or juice and 1 cup plus 2 tablespoons sugar can be applied to any fruit. This sorbet remains creamy in the freezer for up to 2 days.

Apricot Pilaf

I made up this pilaf one day by grabbing bottles from the spice cabinet, and adding the dried fruit and nuts I had on hand.

The result is a Mideast-type pilaf studded with bits of dried apricots and toasted pecans. My friends love it and ask me to make it again and again.

2 tablespoons butter	¼ teaspoon ground mace
1 medium onion, chopped	Salt, pepper
1½ cups long-grain white rice	2 (14½-ounce) cans chicken broth
½ teaspoon cinnamon	½ cup chopped dried apricots
¼ teaspoon fresh-ground nutmeg	½ cup pecan halves
¼ teaspoon ground cardamom	

Melt butter over medium heat in a 6-quart saucepan. Slowly sauté onion in butter until limp. Add rice and stir well to coat. Cook and stir for 2 minutes.

Stir in cinnamon, nutmeg, cardamom, mace, salt and pepper. Add broth. Stir in apricots. Bring to a boil, reduce heat, cover and simmer for 20 minutes, or until rice is tender and broth has been absorbed.

While rice simmers, spread pecan halves on a cookie sheet and toast at 350 degrees for 5 minutes.

Chop toasted pecans. When rice is done, stir pecans into pilaf.

Makes 6 servings.

Pennsylvania Pot Roast

Hands down, this is the best pot roast I've ever tasted. The dill pickle spears contribute a hint of acid to the rich gravy and, surprisingly, taste pretty good after they're cooked. Helen Baughman of Cuyahoga Falls shared the recipe for a newspaper article in 1989.

1 blade pot roast, 2 inches thick (3 to 5 pounds)
Salt, pepper, paprika, flour
½ pound bacon, diced
4 to 6 dill pickle spears
1 large onion, sliced
1 (8-ounce) can tomato sauce
1 cup water
½ cup sour cream

Rub pot roast all over with salt, pepper, paprika and flour. Fry diced bacon in a Dutch oven until crisp. Remove bacon with slotted spoon and drain on paper towels. Pour off all but 3 tablespoons of bacon fat.

Brown pot roast in remaining bacon fat. Add pickles and onion slices. Stir in tomato sauce and water. Cover and simmer for 2½ to 3 hours, adding water if needed. Liquid should come halfway up the side of the roast.

When meat is tender, remove to a platter. Add bacon bits to broth. Stir in sour cream and heat gently. Pass sauce in a gravy boat.

Jane Snow Cooks

Grilled Chicken Under Bricks

The Italian technique of cooking a chicken under bricks usually involves a stove and a frying pan. When I adapted the method for a grill, the results were spectacular—firm, juicy meat with crackling-crisp skin, perfumed with sage and smoke.

1 whole chicken, about 3 to 4 pounds

2 quarts water

½ cup kosher salt

8 to 10 fresh sage leaves

Softened butter

2 lumps hickory or other hard wood, soaked in water

Wash chicken inside and out. Place water and salt in a container large enough to submerge chicken. Stir until salt dissolves. Place chicken in container and add water, if necessary, to cover. Weight down with a plate and refrigerate for at least 2 hours.

Build a hot charcoal fire in one half of a grill. Remove chicken from brine and rinse well. Pat dry with paper towels. With poultry shears or a sharp knife, split chicken in half lengthwise down the center of the breasts. Press chicken as flat as possible.

Gently loosen skin on breasts and tuck sage leaves between skin and breast. Do the same with the thighs. Rub skin all over with softened butter. Put soaked wood on coals. Place chicken on grill directly over the hot coals. Cook uncovered for about 5 minutes, until very brown. Turn and brown other side.

Move chicken to opposite side of grill, away from the coals. Place skinside down. Place an oblong baking pan directly on chicken and weight with 2 bricks. Cover grill with vented lid. Cook for 20 to 25 minutes longer, until juices run clear when the thigh is cut in the thickest part. Transfer to a platter and let stand about 10 minutes before carving.

Makes 4 servings.

Szechuan Stir-Fry Sauce

A jar of this sauce is always in my refrigerator, ready to add bold flavors to last-minute stir fries. Multiply the amounts and make a big batch. It keeps for weeks when refrigerated.

1 tablespoon hoisin sauce
1 tablespoon hot bean sauce
1¼ teaspoons grated fresh ginger
1 tablespoon soy sauce
1 tablespoon sherry
1½ teaspoons rice wine vinegar or distilled white vinegar
1½ teaspoons Asian sesame oil
¾ teaspoon sugar

Combine all ingredients and mix well. Add at end of cooking along with 1 teaspoon cornstarch dissolved in 2 tablespoons water. Stir-fry 1 to 2 minutes longer. May be mixed in larger quantities and stored in a lidded jar in refrigerator.

Makes enough for 1 or 2 stir-fries.

Roasted Tomato Sauce

This is such an easy tomato sauce to make, and it's bursting with flavor. Whole tomatoes, garlic and a halved onion are roasted on a cookie sheet, puréed and then simmered until thick. Roasting intensifies the tomato flavor.

1½ pounds ripe tomatoes (4 large or 6 medium)
4 large cloves garlic, unpeeled
1 medium onion, peeled and cut in half
Salt, pepper
2 tablespoons freshly grated Parmesan

Spray a jelly roll pan (a cookie sheet with sides) with nonstick spray. Place whole tomatoes, garlic cloves and onion halves on tray. Roast at 400 degrees for 20 minutes, or until tomatoes are soft and the skins are just beginning to split. Remove from oven and cool slightly. Remove skins from garlic, squeezing pulp into a blender or the bowl of a food processor. Add onions. Peel tomatoes, discarding skins. Place tomatoes in blender. Purée vegetables until smooth. Pour tomato purée into a saucepan and simmer over medium heat, stirring often, for 20 minutes, or until thick. Season to taste with salt and pepper. Stir in the Parmesan.

This is a very thick sauce. It may be frozen but not canned.

Toffee-Topped Fruitcake

One holiday season, I set out to clone a handful of the most expensive, luscious-looking cakes from mail-order catalogs. The big hit was a fruitcake that's actually more candy than cake. The fruits and nuts are held together with a wisp of batter, and the top is drizzled with liquid toffee that sets to a golden crunch.

Cake

¾ pound walnuts halves
¾ pound pecan halves
1 pound candied red cherries
1 pound candied pineapple chunks
¾ cup flour
¾ cup sugar
½ teaspoon salt
½ teaspoon baking powder
3 eggs

Toffee syrup

1 cup sugar
4 tablespoons butter
½ cup plus 2 tablespoons water

For the cakes: In a large bowl, stir together the walnuts, pecans, cherries and pineapple. In another bowl, whisk together the flour, sugar, salt and baking powder until mixed well. Pour the flour mixture over the fruit and nuts and stir to coat evenly. Beat the eggs until frothy and pour over the fruits and nuts. Mix well with hands.

Generously butter three 8-inch round cake pans. By hand, press the fruit mixture into the pans. Bake at 350 degrees for 40 minutes, until cakes just begin to brown. Cool for 10 minutes, then remove from pans.

For the toffee syrup: While cakes are cooling, combine toffee ingredients in a heavy-bottomed saucepan. Cook and stir over medium heat until the sugar has dissolved, about 10 minutes. Boil without stirring until the mixture reaches the soft-crack stage, 290 degrees on a candy thermometer.

Remove toffee syrup from heat. Working quickly, drizzle over the three fruitcakes. Let stand until firm. Wrap tightly to store.

Makes 3 cakes.

Szechuan Ribs with Hot Chili Oil

With a little knowledge and a covered grill, anyone can make outstanding ribs. To take ribs to the next level, though, you need a great recipe, and this is it. Smoke and heat seal in the gingery marinade and turn the meat a deep molasses brown. A slightly sweet, slightly hot Asian sauce is brushed on at the end.

Marinade

½ cup soy sauce

½ cup dry sherry

¼ cup vegetable oil

1 teaspoon Asian sesame oil

5 quarter-sized pieces of ginger, smashed

2 cloves garlic, smashed

4 pounds spare ribs

Sauce

½ cup hoisin sauce

¼ cup soy sauce

¼ cup sugar

2 tablespoons Asian sesame oil

A few drops of Szechuan hot chili oil, to taste

Combine marinade ingredients and pour over ribs in a 9-by-12-inch pan or an oversized zipper-lock plastic bag. Ribs should be in a single layer in pan or bag. Cover and refrigerate about 4 hours, turning occasionally. Meanwhile, combine sauce ingredients in a small bowl.

Build a large charcoal fire on one side of a grill. When coals have ashed over, remove ribs from marinade and place on grid on other side of grill, away from the coals. Make sure none of the meat is directly over the fire. Open vents in grill bottom and lid. Cover and cook for 30 minutes, turning and changing position of ribs every 10 minutes to promote even cooking. Do this quickly so as little heat as possible escapes.

After 30 minutes, brush ribs on both sides with sauce. Close lid and grill 10 minutes longer. Brush again with sauce, turn and grill 5 to 10 minutes longer. Remove from grill, cut into portions and brush again with sauce.

Makes 4 to 6 servings.

Peach Meringue Pie

In this pie, a rich custard filling is delicately flavored with puréed, canned peaches and topped with a cloud of puffy meringue. I've included two methods for making meringue, both of which eliminate any bacteria present in the egg whites.

1 9-inch baked pie shell	4 egg yolks
¾ cup sugar	1 (15-ounce) can sliced peaches
2½ tablespoons flour	1 tablespoon butter
2 tablespoons cornstarch	¼ teaspoon vanilla extract
¼ teaspoon salt	Meringue topping (recipe follows)
2 cups milk	

Prepare pie shell and set aside. In a medium saucepan, combine sugar, flour, cornstarch and salt; stir well.

In a bowl, combine milk and egg yolks; stir well. Drain peaches thoroughly and pat dry with paper towels. Purée in a blender or food processor. You should have about ¾ to 1 cup. Stir into milk-egg mixture.

Slowly add milk mixture to sugar mixture, stirring until smooth. Stir constantly over medium heat until mixture thickens and comes to a full boil. Stir and boil for 1 minute. Remove from heat and stir in butter and vanilla. Pour hot filling into pie shell.

Make meringue. While filling is still hot, use a knife or spatula to seal meringue to rim of pie shell. Pile remaining meringue onto filling and swirl. For uncooked meringue, bake at 300 degrees for 16 to 18 minutes to kill any potential bacteria. For cooked meringue, bake at 400 degrees for 5 minutes, until golden. Cool for 1 hour at room temperature, then chill thoroughly before cutting.

Makes 1 pie.

Meringue

4 egg whites
¼ teaspoon cream of tartar
½ cup superfine sugar

For uncooked meringue: Combine egg whites and cream of tartar in the bowl of an electric mixer. Beat on medium speed until soft peaks form. Beat on high speed while adding sugar 1 tablespoon at a time, until stiff peaks form and sugar is dissolved. To test, rub a small amount of meringue between your fingers. If the mixture is still gritty, continue beating until smooth.

For cooked meringue: Combine egg whites, cream of tartar and sugar in the top of a double boiler (or in a metal mixer bowl). Add 1 tablespoon water. With a hand mixer, beat on low speed over boiling water until mixture reaches 160 degrees on a candy thermometer or instant-read thermometer. Remove from heat and pour into a deep bowl, if necessary. Beat on high speed until stiff peaks form.

The Recipes

Chapter 5
On the Road

We huddled around the car engine like a couple of good old boys discussing the finer points of carburetor adjustment. In reality, we were trying to decide where to wedge a roast.

Tales of cooking food on a car engine had been floating around for years, and a trip from Pittsburgh to Baltimore seemed like a good chance to check them out.

Suzanne Martinson, food editor of the *Pittsburgh Press*, supplied the car. Her little compact Ford Escort engine didn't look roomy enough to accommodate a hot dog, let alone a 2.8-pound hunk of chuck. Finally, we just slapped the oil-wrapped roast on top of a shiny flat thing (the manifold, we learned later) and closed the hood.

About 250 miles into the trip, we whipped into a Bob Evans parking lot in Breezewood, Pa., opened the hood and stood there for a while admiring the steam rising from our dinner. The sliced onions wrapped up with the roast smelled wonderful. We flipped the meat and took off.

Still, we didn't seriously believe on-the-road-roasting would work until we parked the car in Baltimore. When we unwrapped the package, the meat was fork-tender and as flavorful as any we've cooked at home. The weird experiment actually worked.

Friends who are old hands at auto cooking recommend using relatively thin pieces of meat and cooking only on trips of five hours or more. Also, they say the meat must be wrapped in eight to 10 layers of aluminum foil, probably to prevent the juices from dripping on some crucial engine part.

A trip to Chicago is coming up. I have my eye on a nice turkey cutlet.

Persian Chicken Salad Sandwiches

This is the best chicken salad I've ever tasted. When San Francisco chef Joyce Goldstein served it in baby pitas at a food gala, it outshone all the fancy hors d'oeuvres from the San Francisco's top chefs. The flavors—lemon, mint, basil— are bold, and the interplay of crunchy and soft textures is inspired.

½ small onion

2 tablespoons fresh lemon juice

1 teaspoon paprika

2 teaspoons oregano

1 teaspoon finely minced garlic

¼ cup olive oil

Salt, fresh-ground pepper

4 skinless, boneless chicken breast halves
(about 2 pounds)

¼ cup coarse-chopped, toasted walnuts

1 cup lemon dill mayonnaise
(recipe follows)

4 pita bread rounds or 8 mini pitas

8 slices feta cheese, about ⅛-inch thick

16 large mint leaves

16 large basil leaves

16 sprigs watercress, stems removed

Grind onion, lemon juice, paprika, oregano and garlic in a food processor or blender. Pour into a glass or enamel bowl. Stir in the olive oil; season with salt and pepper. Toss chicken in mixture and marinate in the refrigerator overnight.

Broil chicken breast in a preheated broiler for about 3 minutes on each side. When cool enough to handle, cut into ½-inch cubes. Fold chicken and walnuts into the lemon dill mayonnaise. Chill.

Cut pita loaves in half and open the pockets. Place feta cheese chunks and herb leaves in the pockets. Spoon in chicken salad.

Makes 4 servings.

Lemon Dill Mayonnaise

1 teaspoon grated lemon rind

1 tablespoon fresh lemon juice

2 tablespoons chopped fresh dill

1 cup mayonnaise

Combine all ingredients and mix well. Refrigerate.

Chicago-Style Hot Dogs

The gloriously garnished Chicago-style dog has been around since at least the 1930s, when they were listed on menu boards as Depression sandwiches. All-beef franks are slipped into a poppy seed bun and topped with bright-green sweet relish, mustard, chopped onions, sliced tomatoes, pickled serrano peppers (called "sport peppers"), a dill pickle spear and a dash of celery salt. Some hot dog joints add sliced cucumbers to help counteract the heat of the pepper.

1 all-beef hot dog per person
1 poppy seed hot dog bun (if available) per person
1 teaspoon yellow mustard
1 teaspoon bright-green sweet relish (add a drop of food coloring)
1 teaspoon chopped onions
1 dill pickle spear
2 tomato half-slices
2 small pickled hot peppers
Dash of celery salt

Cook the hot dogs in boiling water. Place each dog in a steamed bun and pile on the toppings in the order listed. Serve immediately with plenty of napkins.

Jane Snow Cooks

Gertie's Crab Cakes

Oh, how cruel to live in the heartland when a crab cake craving comes on. Like pioneers, we do what we have to do. We buy blue crab if we can find it, snow crab if we can't, and surimi fake crab if time is short or funds are low. I brought this recipe back from a crab cake-intensive trip to Baltimore. It's the last word on crab cakes.

1 egg
2 tablespoons mayonnaise (4 tablespoons for snow or surimi crab meat)
1 teaspoon dry mustard
½ teaspoon black pepper
1 teaspoon Old Bay seasoning
2 teaspoons Worcestershire sauce
Dash Tabasco sauce
1 pound crab meat (preferably blue crab)
¼ cup cracker crumbs
Vegetable oil for frying

In a blender or mixing bowl, combine the egg, mayonnaise, mustard, pepper, Old Bay, Worcestershire and Tabasco. Mix until frothy.

Place crab meat in a bowl and pour mixture over the top. Sprinkle on cracker crumbs. Gently toss together with hands, taking care not to break up the lumps of crab meat.

Form mixture by hand into four cakes, or scoop up with an ice cream scoop and pat into 1-inch-thick mounds. Do not pack together too firmly.

Heat about 1 inch of oil to 375 degrees in a deep skillet. Deep-fry crab cakes, a few at a time, until golden brown on both sides, about 3 minutes. Remove with a slotted utensil to paper towels to drain. Serve at once.

Makes 4 servings.

Nid D'abeilles (Bee Sting Cake)

Dome-shaped brioche (sweet bread) stuffed with custard and glossed with honey and sliced almonds is a specialty of the honey-producing area of France's Loire Valley I visited in 2002. One taste and I was a goner. When I returned home I created this version from that sweet memory.

Brioche

6 envelopes active dry yeast
½ cup water
½ cup sugar
2 teaspoons salt
½ cup warm milk
6 egg yolks
3 whole eggs
4 cups (about) unbleached flour
½ pound unsalted butter at room temperature
1 egg yolk beaten with 1 tablespoon water
¼ cup sliced almonds
1 tablespoon honey stirred with 1 teaspoon warm water

Custard filling

2 eggs
2 egg yolks
1½ cups sugar
⅔ cup flour
2 cups boiling milk
4 tablespoons butter
2 tablespoons vanilla extract

For the brioche: The day before serving, sprinkle yeast over warm water. Add a pinch of sugar and stir well. Let stand until the mixture foams, about 5 minutes. Pour into a large mixer bowl with the sugar, salt, milk, yolks and eggs. Mix well. Add a cup of the flour and the butter. Beat well. Slowly add 2 or more cups of flour, beating until a very soft dough forms.

Turn dough onto a lightly floured surface. With floured hands, knead dough until it forms a glossy ball with no stickiness. The dough will be sticky at first, but avoid adding flour if possible.

Place dough in a lightly greased bowl. Cover and let rise in a warm place until doubled in bulk, about 1½ hours. Punch down and return to bowl. Cover with plastic wrap and refrigerate overnight.

Remove dough from refrigerator and punch down. Divide in half. Roll each piece into a 10-inch circle. Fit into the bottom of 10-inch springform pans. Cover with a dish towel and let rise until almost doubled in bulk.

Brush tops of loaves with the egg-water mixture. Sprinkle sliced almonds over tops. Bake at 425 degrees for about 20 minutes, or until golden brown. Cool in pans, then remove sides of pans. Brush tops with the honey mixture.

For the custard: Beat eggs and yolks with an electric mixer, slowly adding sugar until mixture is pale yellow and forms a ribbon when dropped from a beater. Beat in flour. Beat in milk in a very thin stream.

Pour into a heavy-bottomed saucepan. Cook and stir with a whisk over medium heat until mixture coagulates. Remove from heat and whisk rapidly until smooth. Over low heat, beat 2 to 3 minutes to cook the flour. Remove from heat and beat in butter and vanilla. Chill.

To assemble: With a serrated bread knife, cut loaves in half horizontally. Fill each with half of the chilled custard. Cut into wedges to serve.

Makes 2 loaves. Store in refrigerator.

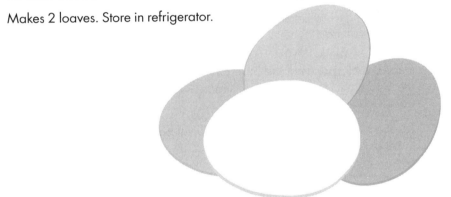

Gazpacho Andalucia

My gazpacho "aha!" moment came at a seaside café in Spain. The chilled soup was a creamy coral instead of the usual bright-red, and blessedly lacked the jangly acid edge of puréed raw tomatoes. The secret was plain old bread, whirled in the blender with the vegetables. The soup was smooth, not chunky. It came with tiny bowls of chopped vegetables, to be added by the diner at the table.

1 cup plus 2 tablespoons extra-virgin olive oil

½ cup minced onion

½ cup dry white wine

4 ounces stale bread (¼ of a 1-pound loaf)

2 pounds very ripe tomatoes (about 5 medium-large)

1 medium green bell pepper, seeded and cut into chunks

3 large cloves garlic, peeled

6 tablespoons white wine vinegar

2 teaspoons salt

1 cup peeled, diced cucumber

1 cup diced onion

1 cup diced red bell pepper

1 cup diced tomato

Heat 2 tablespoons of the olive oil in a medium skillet. Sauté ½ cup of the onions until limp. Add wine, turn heat to high and boil until wine is reduced to ¼ cup.

Scrape cooked onion-wine mixture into the bowl of a food processor. Remove crusts from bread and tear bread into chunks; add half to food processor. Remove skin from tomatoes, cut in half horizontally and squeeze out seeds. Cut tomatoes into chunks and add half to food processor. Add half of the green pepper chunks, garlic, vinegar and salt.

With motor running, pour half of the remaining olive oil through feed tube, puréeing mixture until very smooth. Scrape mixture into a bowl or pitcher. Repeat with remaining half of bread, tomatoes, bell pepper chunks, garlic, vinegar, oil and salt. Combine the two batches of soup and chill for at least 1 hour.

Ladle soup into chilled bowls. Serve cucumber, diced onion, red bell pepper and tomato in separate bowls, to add to the soup at the table.

Makes 6 servings.

Steak with Spinach-Chipotle Pepper Sauce

Pan-broiled steak topped with a creamy spinach and chipotle pepper sauce is a special-occasion treat. My recipe is based on a dish I tasted at a restaurant in Cozumel, Mexico. Chipotle peppers in adobo sauce are ripe jalapeño peppers smoked and canned in a thick, brick-red liquid.

Salt
2 boneless steaks, less than 1-inch thick
½ tablespoon butter
1 teaspoon minced onion
¼ cup dry vermouth or any other dry, white wine
1 cup cream
⅓ box frozen, chopped spinach, thawed and squeezed dry
⅓ of a canned chipotle pepper, minced

Heat a heavy, well-seasoned skillet over high heat. Sprinkle salt over bottom. Place steaks in pan and sear for 1 minute over high heat. Turn steaks and reduce heat to medium-low. Cook uncovered for 5 minutes, turning once, for medium-rare.

Remove steaks from skillet and keep warm. Melt butter in skillet and sauté onion for 1 minute over medium heat. Increase heat to high, add vermouth and boil until reduced by half. Add cream, stir and bring to a boil. Boil for 1 minute. Stir in remaining ingredients and continue to boil until heated through and cream is reduced by about half. Spoon sauce over steaks.

Makes 2 servings.

Nectarine-Blackberry Cobbler

On a food expedition to Oregon I enjoyed the local berries in a dozen different ways, but none more luscious than a blackberry and nectarine cobbler. Portland chef Greg Higgins crowned the fruit with a crunchy, buttery crust and served it with pitchers of pouring custard.

Filling

2 pints blackberries

6 nectarines, peeled and sliced

Juice of 1 lemon

½ teaspoon salt

1 cup granulated sugar

¼ cup brown sugar

1 teaspoon vanilla extract

¼ cup flour

1 teaspoon mace

Topping

12 tablespoons (1½ sticks) butter, softened

¾ cup sugar

1 teaspoon vanilla extract

3 eggs

1 cup flour

1½ teaspoons baking powder

¼ teaspoon salt

For the filling: Place all but ½ pint berries in a bowl. Combine with remaining filling ingredients. Toss gently. Set aside while making cobbler batter.

For the topping: With an electric mixer, cream butter and sugar until fluffy. Add vanilla. Add eggs one at a time, scraping down sides of bowl after each addition. Sift together dry ingredients. Add to creamed mixture, mixing just until combined. Fold in remaining half-pint berries.

Place fruit mixture in a buttered, 9-by-12-inch baking pan. With a spoon, dollop batter over fruit (don't worry about distributing it evenly). Bake at 350 degrees for 45 minutes, or until top is golden brown and fruit is bubbling. Serve warm or at room temperature with English Pouring Custard.

English Pouring Custard

¾ cup sugar

8 egg yolks

½ gallon whipping cream (8 half-pints)

1 tablespoon vanilla extract

Lemon juice to taste

With a mixer, beat sugar and egg yolks until fluffy. Bring cream to a simmer. Add to egg mixture in a thin stream, beating with mixer. Return to saucepan. Heat over low heat until mixture thickens, stirring constantly. Do not bring to a simmer or the eggs will curdle. Remove from heat. Stir in vanilla and a splash of lemon juice. Chill. Serve with cobbler or over fresh fruit.

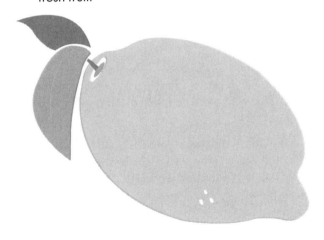

Stuffed Sopaipillas

Sopaipillas are triangles of dough that puff dramatically when deep-fried. In New Mexico, the flaky triangles can be found in bread baskets or topped with a chile-spiced pork mixture called carne adovada. The meat mixture also makes a mean burrito. My recipe was created when a craving hit after a trip to the Southwest.

> 2 cups flour
> 2 teaspoons baking powder
> ½ teaspoon salt
> ¼ cup vegetable shortening
> ⅔ cup water (or more as needed)
> Vegetable oil for deep-frying
> Carne adovada (recipe follows)

Stir together flour, baking powder and salt in a bowl. Add shortening in small hunks and cut into the flour with a pastry blender, as for pie dough. Add water a little at a time, tossing with a fork to make a soft dough. The dough should be smooth, but not sticky.

Gently gather dough into a ball; do not press or knead. Divide into two pieces. On a floured board, roll each piece into a circle about ⅛-inch thick. Cut each circle into six or eight pie-shaped wedges.

Heat about 2 inches of oil in a heavy, deep skillet until very hot. Fry a few dough wedges at a time until brown on both sides. Drain on paper towels.

To serve, place two sopaipillas on each plate and top with some of the carne adovada.

Makes 8 to 10 servings.

Carne Adovada

3 ounces dried New Mexican red chili peppers

4 cloves garlic, minced

3 teaspoons dried oregano

3 cups water

4 pounds pork, cut into 1-inch cubes

Remove stems from chile peppers. Tear into chunks and place with seeds in a food processor or blender. Process until most of the pepper has been reduced to powder, with a few chunks here and there. You should have about ¾ cup. Add garlic, oregano and water and pulse briefly to mix.

Place pork cubes in a large, shallow casserole dish (a lasagna pan works well). Pour chili mixture over meat and mix well. Cover and refrigerate several hours or overnight. Uncover and bake at 300 degrees for 2 to 3 hours, until pork is very tender and starts to fall apart.

Mixture may be used for stuffed sopaipillas or as a filling for burritos or enchiladas. Leftovers may be frozen.

Beef & Stilton Cornish Pasties

A trip to Cornwall in England inspired me to recreate the meat turnovers indigenous to the region. Decades ago when tin miners toted the hand-held meal to work, pasties were made with ground beef and turnips, period. Now the region's bakers create pasties with a variety of upscale fillings, including this one.

1 recipe pastry (recipe follows)
4 ounces beef chuck steak, cut in ¼-inch cubes
½ medium turnip, peeled and cubed
1 medium potato, peeled and sliced thin
Salt, pepper
½ medium onion, chopped
2 ounces Stilton cheese, crumbled
1 tablespoon butter, in small pieces
1 egg beaten with 1 tablespoon milk

Divide pastry in half and roll each half into a circle about 8 or 9 inches in diameter. Use a luncheon plate of the proper size, if available, as a guide for cutting the dough into an even circle.

Place meat in a small bowl. Place turnip and potatoes in another small bowl and toss.

On the bottom half of each pastry circle, arrange a layer of turnips and potatoes. Season with salt and pepper. Arrange the meat over the potatoes on each pastry circle. Season with salt and pepper. Top with onions, then cheese. Finish with another layer of turnips and potatoes.

Season the top layer with salt and pepper and dot with butter. Moisten the edges of the pastry with water. Fold the pastry over the filling to form half moons, pressing the edges to seal. Crimp the edges.

Place pasties on a lightly greased baking sheet. Brush tops with the egg mixture. Bake at 450 degrees for 10 minutes. Reduce temperature to 300 degrees and bake 40 minutes longer.

Makes 2 pasties.

Pastry

2 cups flour
½ teaspoon salt
4 tablespoons chilled butter
4 tablespoons chilled vegetable shortening
5 tablespoons water

In a food processor, combine flour and salt and process briefly. Drop small pieces of butter and then shortening through the feed tube, pulsing briefly after each addition. Process for a minute or so to thoroughly distribute fat.

With the motor running, trickle the water through the feed tube, adding just enough to make the dough clump together. The dough should be stiff but not dry.

Makes enough dough for 2 pasties.

Goulaschsuppe

This is my version of the bone-warming, chunky soup I enjoyed on a ski vacation in Austria. The soup is handed out to skiers from windows in mountainside food huts, and diners sip it outdoors, sitting on lawn chairs in the snow. The key to achieving the proper texture is cutting the vegetables into precise little cubes. The vegetable-beef soup is seasoned with caraway.

2 tablespoons butter

2 tablespoons oil

2 pounds lean beef chuck or round, cut in ¾ inch cubes

Salt, pepper

2 medium onions, chopped

1 green pepper, chopped fine

2 cloves garlic, minced

2 tablespoons sweet Hungarian paprika

1 (16-ounce) can whole plum tomatoes, drained and chopped fine

¼ teaspoon caraway seeds

1 bay leaf

2 (14½-ounce) cans beef broth

1 cup water

2 medium potatoes, finely diced

2 carrots, finely diced

Heat butter and oil over high heat in a heavy soup kettle. Season beef with salt and pepper. In batches, brown beef cubes in hot oil; remove with a slotted spoon and reserve.

Reduce heat to low. In same kettle, cook onions, green pepper and garlic for 15 minute, stirring occasionally. Add paprika and cook and stir for 2 minutes.

Return beef and any collected juices to kettle. Add remaining ingredients. Bring to a boil, reduce heat, cover and simmer over low heat for 45 minutes, until beef and vegetables are tender. Season to taste with salt and pepper.

Makes 6 servings.

Jane Snow Cooks

Pickled Grapes

An antipasto platter was punctuated with these unusual, delicious marinated grapes at a lunch in California's Carneros Valley wine region. The recipe is from Sonoma caterer Elaine Bell.

2 pounds seedless red grapes, stemmed

2 cups rose or raspberry wine vinegar
   (may substitute 1 cup any red vinegar and 1 cup white wine vinegar)

1 cup dry red wine

1¼ cups sugar

4 whole cloves

1 cinnamon stick

6 cardamom seeds, crushed

1 sprig fresh tarragon

Place grapes in a 2-quart jar. Combine remaining ingredients in a heavy, nonreactive saucepan over medium heat, stirring until sugar is dissolved. Cool slightly, then pour over grapes.

Cover tightly and refrigerate for 2 days before using, inverting jar occasionally to make sure grapes are evenly marinated. Grapes will keep up to 10 days in the refrigerator but should be removed from marinade so that the flavors do not become too strong.

Serve as a garnish with an entrée, on an antipasto plate or as an hors d'oeuvre.

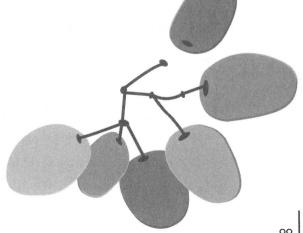

White Chocolate Banana Cream Pie

I knew it was a winner with the first bite, but I ate the rest of the slice just to be certain. I ordered the pie—and later got the recipe—at the marvelous Buckhead Diner in Atlanta while attending a food conference. If I get to choose my last meal on earth, this will be the dessert.

Crust

1 cup (2 sticks) butter
¾ cup sugar
1 egg
2½ cups flour

Garnish

12 ounces white chocolate for curls
Unsweetened cocoa powder

Pastry cream

6 egg yolks
5 tablespoons sugar
¼ cup cornstarch
2 cups milk
1 vanilla bean, cut in half
2 tablespoons butter, cut up
3 ounces white chocolate, melted

Banana cream filling

8 ripe bananas
Juice of 1 lemon
2 cups whipping cream, chilled
3 tablespoons white crème de cacao
3 tablespoons banana liqueur

For the crust: In large bowl, blend butter and sugar; do not cream. Add egg and incorporate completely. Add flour and mix for 2 minutes with the dough hook of an electric mixer, or mix thoroughly with a pastry blender. Wrap with plastic wrap and refrigerate 2 hours.

Divide dough in half and quickly roll out half the dough on a floured surface to a ¼-inch-thick circle. Fit into a 10-inch tart pan (a pie pan with straight sides). Repeat with remaining dough. Refrigerate 30 minutes.

Heat oven to 350 degrees. Bake pie shells for 12 to 16 minutes. Cool on wire racks.

For the pastry cream: In a medium bowl, whisk egg yolks and sugar until pale yellow. Whisk in cornstarch. In a saucepan, bring milk and vanilla bean to a boil; remove from heat and remove vanilla bean.

Stir a small amount of hot milk into the egg mixture. Return milk to heat and while stirring, slowly add the egg mixture. Continue stirring until mixture thickens. Allow to just come to a boil, remove from heat and stir in butter. Put mixture through a sieve into a bowl and cover with plastic wrap. Cool slightly, then stir in melted white chocolate. Cover and refrigerate until ready to assemble pie.

For the banana cream filling: Slice bananas and toss with the lemon juice. Whip cream until stiff peaks form; fold in pastry cream, then fold in bananas and liqueurs. Fill tart shells with filling.

For the white chocolate curls: Draw a vegetable peeler across the broad, flat surface of a room-temperature (about 80 degrees) chunk of white chocolate to make large, thin curls. (Can be made earlier and refrigerated.)

Top pies generously with white chocolate curls, then dust with cocoa. Serve soon after assembling to keep from becoming soggy.

Makes 2 pies.

The Recipes

Chapter 6
Appetizers

S omewhere in America, folks dine on picnics of chilled oysters, cold squab, and petit fours. I wish they'd send me an invitation. The people I know—and probably you, too—celebrate with down-home gusto. They dress down, lounge around and eat potluck dishes that were thrown together the night before. Someone usually brings supermarket potato salad masquerading as homemade.

My cousin once smeared the icing on a store-bought cake and passed it off as her own until we discovered the telltale cardboard base. We still rib her about it and kind of admire her, too. Wish we had thought of it.

But I have my own sneaky game plan for picnic and party potluck. I take appetizers. No matter what they are, people gobble them up because they're the only game in town until the main picnic debuts. You could toss Spam and cheese cubes on a paper plate and people would be grateful.

In about the time it takes to refrost a bakery cake, you could heat pineapple preserves with some ginger and soy sauce, pour it over some pork riblets, spread them on a cookie sheet and pop them in the oven. For five minutes of work, tops, you'd have a terrific appetizer.

I've got dozens of these quickie recipes. The defining elements are speed and guilt. I don't want to cook, so I make it fast. I don't have the guts to take carry-out potato salad, so I make it homemade.

The result is—voila!—darling little bite-sized taco salads. Tiny phyllo shells from the store freezer case are filled with a dab of cream cheese, a dab of salsa, a pinch of chopped lettuce and a black olive ring.

Or cucumbers are cut into chunky, 1½-inch thick rounds and the top is sliced at an angle. With a melon baller, a depression is made in the top, and filled with sour cream and a sprinkling of inexpensive caviar.

You're probably thinking, "Well, I make quick appetizers, too. I put a block of cream cheese on a plate and douse it with cocktail sauce and canned shrimp." Get over it.

Instead, make an appetizer that actually tastes great, such as Kung Bao Shells. I dreamed this one up in desperation a few years ago when all I had on hand was chicken, peanuts and pasta. The shells are wonderfully quirky containers for the spicy chicken stir-fry. The appetizers can be eaten by hand, and taste good both at room temperature and cold.

My friends who brought carryout loved them.

Bangkok Wings

Hot wings with a Southeast Asian flavor were popular at Bangkok Gourmet Restaurant in Akron. Although the eatery is gone, you can still enjoy these fiery, hot-sweet wings with this recipe from the restaurant.

½ cup sesame oil

1 cup butter or margarine

3 heads garlic, peeled and crushed

3 tablespoons paprika

½ cup rice wine

¼ cup teriyaki sauce

1 gallon Thai red chili sauce (available at Asian markets)

¾ cup honey

2 tablespoons black pepper

100 chicken wing pieces

Oil for deep-frying

Place sesame oil and butter in a large kettle over low heat until butter is melted. Add garlic and lightly brown. Add paprika, rice wine and teriyaki sauce; boil for 2 minutes. Add chili sauce and continue to cook over low heat for about 15 minutes, stirring frequently and allowing to gradually thicken. Add honey and black pepper and cook and stir for several minutes.

Heat oil to 375 to 400 degrees. Drop in wings a few at a time and cook for about 7 to 10 minutes, depending on size. The wings will rise to the top when they are almost done. Drain well on paper towels.

Place hot wings and enough sauce to coat in a lidded container. Cover tightly and shake well.

Makes 100.

Vietnamese Pork in Lettuce Leaves

Little logs of seasoned ground pork are grilled on skewers, then snuggled in lettuce leaves with sprigs of fresh mint. Serve the lettuce and herbs on one platter and the pork skewers on another, and invite dinners to assemble the snacks themselves. It's a good ice-breaker for a party, and the bright, intense flavors are stunning.

1 pound ground pork	½ teaspoon peeled and minced fresh ginger
1 large clove garlic, minced	½ teaspoon cayenne pepper
1 minced green onion, including top	Pinch sugar
1 tablespoon soy sauce	⅛ teaspoon salt
2 teaspoons vegetable oil	20 Bibb lettuce leaves
1½ teaspoons lemon juice	Fresh mint leaves

In bowl, combine all ingredients except lettuce and mint leaves. Mix gently but thoroughly with fingertips and form into 20 sausage-shaped logs about three inches long and one-half inch thick. Chill.

Thread meat on bamboo skewers that have been soaked in water, two pieces of meat per skewer. Grill on a charcoal grill or broil until cooked through.

To serve, slide pork logs off skewers and ask guests to place a pork log and 2 mint leaves in a Bibb lettuce leaf. Wrap to form a neat packet, and dip into the sauce.

Makes 6 servings as an appetizer, 4 as a main course.

Dipping Sauce

¼ cup soy sauce

2 tablespoons lemon juice

1 tablespoon water

1 clove garlic, minced

1 teaspoon sugar

1 teaspoon minced fresh ginger

¼ teaspoon cayenne pepper

Combine all ingredients and let stand for several hours before serving. Serve in small bowls for dipping.

Kung Bao Shells

I dreamed up these flavorful bites one day when I had some peanuts, pasta and chicken on hand, and a potluck picnic in the offing. I transformed a classic Szechuan stir fry into finger food, and friends gobbled them up.

24 jumbo pasta shells	3 tablespoons vegetable oil
3 boneless chicken breast halves	2 dried Szechuan chili peppers
2 teaspoons cornstarch	½ of a red bell pepper, diced
1 teaspoon sesame oil	⅔ cup peanuts
1 tablespoon sherry	3 green onions, sliced
1 tablespoon soy sauce	Sauce (recipe follows)

Cook pasta in boiling water for 10 minutes, or until tender-firm. Do not overcook. (It's a good idea to cook a few extra in case shells split). Rinse under cold water and drain, open-side down, on a kitchen towel.

Cut chicken into bite-sized pieces and place in a medium bowl. Sprinkle cornstarch, sesame oil, sherry and soy sauce over chicken; mix well.

Heat oil in large skillet over medium-high heat. Add dried peppers and stir-fry until peppers turn dark; remove and discard. Add bell pepper and stir-fry for 1 minute. Add green onions and chicken and stir-fry until chicken is barely cooked through. Add sauce and stir and cook until thickened. Stir in peanuts. Remove from heat.

Fill shells with chicken mixture. Arrange on a plate and cover with plastic wrap. Refrigerate until serving time. Serve cold or at room temperature.

Makes 24 appetizers.

Jane Snow Cooks

Sauce

2 teaspoons hoisin sauce

1 teaspoon Chinese hot bean sauce

1 teaspoon soy sauce

1 teaspoon sherry

½ teaspoon rice vinegar

½ teaspoon sesame oil

¼ teaspoon sugar

Combine all ingredients and mix well.

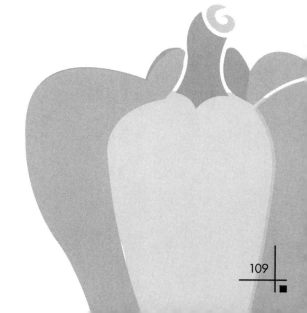

Moroccan Meatballs

Let's assume you have no hired help. Let's assume you don't want to spend days stuffing goat cheese into weensy snow pea pods. Let's assume you actually have a life. The solution is Moroccan Meatballs. They're baked in big batches on cookie sheets, and they taste fabulous. They're scented with cinnamon, sweetened with brown sugar and studded with golden raisins.

1 cup converted rice
3 pounds ground chuck
1 small onion, minced
1½ teaspoons salt
¾ teaspoon pepper

¾ teaspoon cinnamon
¼ cup packed brown sugar
3 tablespoons ketchup
1 egg
1⅓ cups golden raisins or dried cranberries

Cook rice according to package directions, omitting the butter.

Meanwhile, combine ground chuck, onion, salt, pepper, cinnamon and brown sugar in a large bowl. With fingertips, separate the meat and distribute the ingredients evenly.

Add ketchup and egg, and gently mix with fingertips. Add raisins and rice and mix again.

Shape mixture into balls the size of walnuts. Place 1 inch apart on jelly roll pans (a cookie sheet with sides). Bake at 375 degrees for 12 minutes. Drain on paper towels. Serve warm or at room temperature.

Makes 6 to 7 dozen.

Baked Brie in Puff Pastry

Make this when you want to dazzle but are pressed for time. After the pastry is thawed, it can be assembled in minutes. An almost infinite number of versions can be made by varying the preserves and nuts. Try spicy jalapeño jelly and pecans or strawberry preserves and walnuts, served with ginger wafers instead of crackers.

1 sheet frozen puff pastry, thawed (½ of a 17.3-ounce box)

1 wheel of Brie, 6 to 8 ounces (about 4 inches in diameter)

3 tablespoons apricot preserves

3 tablespoons (about 1 ounce) slivered, blanched almonds, toasted

1 egg yolk beaten with 1 tablespoon water

Unfold sheet of pastry and gently flatten the creases with a rolling pin.

Place the wheel of cheese on a counter. Spread the preserves on top of the cheese. Sprinkle with nuts. Place the pastry sheet over the cheese and wrap the edges under. Trim off any excess pastry with a sharp knife.

Place on a baking sheet. Cut leaves or other decorations from pastry scraps. Affix them to the top of the pastry-wrapped cheese with the egg yolk mixture. Brush pastry all over with the egg yolk mixture.

Bake at 400 degrees for about 25 minutes, until golden brown. Serve immediately with crackers.

Samosas

These savory deep-fried turnovers are eaten all over India as appetizers and snacks. If you've had samosas in restaurants, you'll be amazed at how much better the homemade version is. The pastry is crisp and flaky, and the filling sings with flavor.

Filling

1 medium potato, peeled and cut in
   ¼-inch dice
2 tablespoons oil
½ cup chopped onion
2 cloves garlic, minced
1 teaspoon grated fresh ginger
½ teaspoon salt
½ teaspoon ground coriander
¼ teaspoon ground cumin
¼ teaspoon turmeric
Dash of cayenne
2 cups frozen peas
2 tablespoons water
1 tablespoon lemon juice
2 tablespoons chopped fresh cilantro

Dough

1 cup flour
½ teaspoon salt
1 tablespoon plus 2 teaspoons oil
5 tablespoons (about) lukewarm water
Oil for deep-frying

For the filling: Cook potato cubes in water to cover until tender; drain.

Heat oil in a large skillet. Sauté onion, garlic and ginger over medium heat until soft. Add salt, coriander, cumin, turmeric and cayenne. Cook and stir for 3 minutes.

Add potatoes and cook about 3 minutes over medium-high heat, stirring. Stir in peas, water and lemon juice. Cover and cook over low heat for 5 minutes. Remove from heat and stir in cilantro. Cool to room temperature.

For the dough: Combine flour, salt and oil in bowl and toss well to distribute oil. Add water a little at a time, stirring until a very soft dough is formed. Knead briefly and shape into a ball.

Pinch off a piece of dough about the size of a walnut. Shape into a ball, then flatten into a disc. On a floured surface, roll into a 5-inch circle. Cut the circle in half.

Place a tablespoon of filling on one of the half-circles. Wet the edges of dough. Fold in half, lining up the straight edge. Pinch straight edge to seal. Bring the center of the curved edge to the point of the sealed straight edge. Pinch dough to seal along the two open seams, to form a pyramid. Continue with remaining dough and filling.

Heat about 3 inches of vegetable oil in a wide, deep kettle until very hot (about 375 degrees). Deep-fry samosas a few at a time until golden. Drain on paper towels. Makes 12.

Note: Both the filling and the dough can be made a day in advance, and the samosas can be deep-fried an hour or two ahead of time and reheated for about 15 minutes in a 350-degree oven.

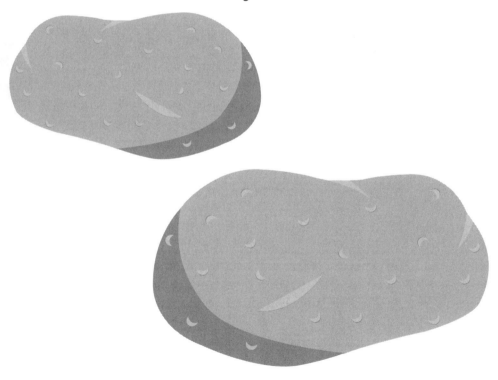

Asparagus & Salmon Spring Rolls

Spring rolls, the delicate little sisters of egg rolls, can be made easily at home. When filled with asparagus and salmon, they're perfect for ushering in spring. The rolls can be made in advance, refrigerated and warmed up in the oven.

3 tablespoons oil

4 spears asparagus, cut in ½-inch lengths

2 green onions, sliced

2 quarter-sized pieces ginger

2 cloves garlic, minced

6 ounces salmon fillet

1 tablespoon soy sauce

1 tablespoon fresh lemon juice

1 tablespoon minced chives

Salt, pepper

12 spring roll wrappers

Oil for deep frying

Spicy Orange Sauce (recipe follows)

Heat oil in a large skillet over medium-high heat. Stir-fry asparagus for 1 minute. Add green onions and stir-fry 30 seconds longer. Remove onions and asparagus from skillet with a slotted spoon and place in a medium bowl.

Cool pan slightly. Smash ginger and garlic with a meat pounder or flat blade of a chef's knife. Place in skillet over medium-high heat. Stir-fry until golden, pressing down on garlic and ginger to release flavors. Remove garlic and ginger and discard.

Place fish in skillet, skin-side up. Cook 5 minutes on each side, or until cooked through. Remove from skillet and cool. Remove skin and flake salmon into medium-sized chunks. Place in bowl with vegetables. Add soy sauce, lemon juice, chives and salt and pepper; mix gently.

Peel a spring roll wrapper from the stack and dip into a bowl of warm water for a few seconds to soften. Place on a kitchen towel and blot dry. Place wrapper on a work surface, with one point facing you if using square wrappers. Place 2 tablespoons of salmon mixture on the lower third of the wrapper. Fold the lower point of the wrapper over the filling and roll once. Fold the sides into the middle. Continue rolling to form a log. Set aside and continue with remaining wrappers.

Heat about 2 inches of oil in a wide, heavy-bottomed pan until very hot. Fry 3 salmon rolls at a time, making sure rolls don't stick together. Fry for about 4 minutes or until golden brown. Drain on paper towels. Serve with Spicy Orange Sauce.

Makes 6 servings.

Spicy Orange Sauce

1 tablespoon minced ginger

1 tablespoon minced orange peel

2 tablespoons hoisin sauce

1 teaspoon Chinese chili sauce

2 tablespoons orange marmalade

½ cup orange juice

Combine all ingredients in a saucepan and boil for 2 minutes to concentrate flavors. Chill.

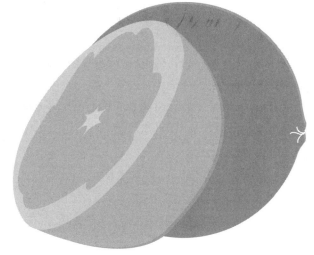

Southwestern Appetizer Tarts

Wonton wrappers are turned into miniature tart shells and filled with taco salad fixings. The pretty little cocktail tidbits take just 20 minutes to make.

24 wonton wrappers

Vegetable oil

1 (8-ounce) package cream cheese, softened

1 teaspoon prepared horseradish

½ teaspoon ground cumin

½ to 1 fresh jalapeño pepper, seeded and minced fine

4 ounces shredded Cheddar cheese

1 medium tomato

Sliced black olives for garnish

Preheat oven to 350 degrees. Brush minimuffin tins (enough tins to make 24 tarts) with oil. Place a wonton wrapper in each cup, flattening wrinkles to the sides of the cups. Brush lightly with oil. Bake at 350 degrees for 10 to 15 minutes, until light brown and crisp.

Meanwhile, beat cream cheese in a bowl with horseradish and cumin until fluffy. Stir in minced jalapeño and Cheddar cheese. Chop tomato and set aside. Slice olives.

When wonton cups are done, remove from oven and fill each cup with a tablespoon or so of the cheese mixture. Top with some chopped tomato and 1 olive slice. May be made a day in advance and refrigerated.

Makes 24.

Authentic Buffalo Chicken Wings

Let's set the record straight: All we're talking about here is three ingredients—chicken, hot sauce and butter. If you're using anything else, you're doing it wrong. This recipe came from a former worker at the Buffalo, N.Y., bar where hot wings originated.

20 to 25 chicken wings
¼ cup butter or margarine
½ to 1 (2½-ounce) bottle Durkee Louisiana Hot Sauce, or to taste
Oil for deep-frying

Cut off and discard the wing tips. Cut main wing bone at joint, separating into 2 pieces. Melt butter, add hot sauce and stir (you may want to double the sauce recipe). Heat oil in a heavy pan or deep fryer until hot (375 to 400 degrees F.). Deep-fry the wings, a few at a time, until cooked through but still juicy. The wings should take 5 to 8 minutes to cook, depending on size.

Transfer to an oven-proof baking dish and keep warm in the oven while frying remaining wings. When all wings have been cooked, pour sauce over wings and stir to coat. Serve with celery stick and blue cheese for dipping.

Makes 4 servings.

Indonesian Chicken Wings

A rich honey-soy sauce glaze elevates these wings above the ordinary. The ingredients are assembled in minutes and then baked for about two hours, making them a convenient snack for a crowd.

3 to 4 dozen chicken wings
1 cup honey
¾ cup soy sauce
¼ cup chopped garlic
½ cup grated fresh ginger

Cut the chicken wings in half at the joint and cut off and discard the wing tips, if desired. Soften the honey by placing the jar in hot water for a few minutes. In a bowl, mix the honey, soy sauce, garlic and ginger.

Arrange the chicken wings in a single layer in a large, shallow pan. Pour sauce over wings, making sure the wings are fully covered. Cover with foil and bake at 325 degrees for 1½ to 2 hours. Uncover pan, increase heat to 375 degrees and bake 45 minutes longer.

When done, the chicken will be a rich, dark brown and the sauce will be reduced by about two-thirds.

Parmesan Shrimp Puffs

A creamy shrimp mixture is piled on rounds of Parmesan-flavored pastry, and baked until puffy and brown. Store-bought refrigerated pie dough makes quick work of this canape.

1 9-inch refrigerated pie crust disk, unbaked

1 egg white beaten with 2 teaspoons water

2 tablespoons Parmesan cheese

1 (4½-ounce) can tiny shrimp

1 or 2 green onions, including tops, sliced

1 teaspoon lemon juice

6 tablespoons mayonnaise

Let pastry disk stand at room temperature according to package directions. Roll out slightly on a floured surface, increasing the diameter by about one-half inch. With a 2-inch cookie cutter or glass, cut out rounds of dough. The pastry should yield about 24.

Place pastry rounds on a baking sheet. Brush with the egg white and sprinkle lightly with 1 tablespoon of the cheese. Prick each round twice with a fork. Bake at 400 degrees for 6 to 8 minutes, until light brown. Cool. Drain shrimp and mash with a fork. Add green onions, lemon juice, mayonnaise and remaining Parmesan cheese. Mix well. Mound onto cooled pastry rounds, spreading to the edges. Bake at 400 degrees for 10 minutes, or until puffy and golden.

Makes 2 dozen.

Pineapple-Ginger Glazed Riblets

These cocktail tidbits require less than five minutes of hands-on preparation, yet they're so good, we bet someone asks how you made them. Don't let on that they were as easy to make as setting out bowls of chips and dip.

3 pounds spareribs
½ of a 12-ounce jar pineapple preserves
¼ cup soy sauce
½ teaspoon powdered ginger

Call ahead and ask the butcher to cut the slab of spareribs into ribs and to cut the ribs into 3-inch pieces. At home, trim off any obvious clumps of fat.

In a small saucepan, combine preserves, soy and ginger. Heat until jelly melts. Pour over ribs in a bowl and stir to coat.

Spread in a single layer on a baking sheet lined with foil. Bake at 425 degrees for 20 to 25 minutes. Serve hot or at room temperature.

Makes about 2 dozen pieces.

Jane Snow Cooks

Grilled Asparagus & Prosciutto

A combination of salty-crisp prosciutto, oozing cheese and smoky asparagus is my favorite finger food. These noshes are a great way to start a cookout.

12 fat spears of asparagus (about 1 pound)
6 thin slices prosciutto (2 ounces)
3 ounces cream cheese, softened
½ cup grated fontina or Swiss cheese (about 2 ounces)

Wash asparagus and trim the tough ends. Place in a large, shallow skillet with about one-half inch hot water. Cover and bring rapidly to a boil. Boil 2 minutes. Drain immediately and cool under cold, running water. Drain and pat dry.

Cut prosciutto slices in half lengthwise, so that each slice produces two long strips. In a small bowl, beat together the cheeses until creamy. Spread about 2 teaspoons of cheese mixture on each strip of prosciutto. Cheese-side in, wrap strips around asparagus stalks in a spiral.

Grill asparagus over hot coals for about 2 minutes, turning once, until prosciutto starts to brown and cheese is bubbly.

Makes 4 servings.

Asian Phyllo Kisses

These bite-sized phyllo kisses are filled with an Asian-flavored stir-fry of chicken, water chestnuts and green onions. They look like they took forever to make, but incorporate several shortcuts such as bottled stir fry sauce.

8 sheets thawed phyllo dough
¾ pound boneless, skinless chicken breast halves
2 tablespoons oil
½ cup sliced green onions
1 (5-ounce) can sliced water chestnuts, in ¼-inch pieces
½ cup bottled stir-fry sauce, any flavor
Butter-flavored oil spray

Thaw phyllo overnight in the refrigerator.

Cut chicken into ¼-inch pieces. Heat oil over high heat in a large skillet. Stir-fry chicken for 1 minute. Add onions and water chestnuts and stir-fry 1 minute longer. Add sauce and stir-fry until liquid has evaporated to a glaze. Set aside.

Peel 2 sheets of phyllo dough from stack, keeping remaining sheets covered with waxed paper and a damp towel. Place the two sheets, one on top of the other, on a work surface. Spray the top sheet with butter-flavored oil spray.

Cut the sheets in half horizontally, then in half vertically. Cut each oblong in half vertically again, to produce 8 oblongs.

Place a teaspoon of the stir-fry in the center of each oblong double-layer of dough. Gather the dough around the filling like a draw-string purse, working gently to prevent tearing the dough. Twist top slightly. Place on a baking sheet and spray the outside with butter-flavored spray. Repeat with remaining dough and filling until filling is used up.

Bake immediately or store the kisses for up to 24 hours on the cookie sheet, uncovered, in the refrigerator. Bake in a preheated, 350-degree oven for 12 to 15 minutes, until golden brown.

Makes about 26.

Tips

For a cocktail party for up to thirty people, two or three varieties of hot hors d'oeuvres are plenty. Figure on about four to six per person, in addition to a spread and some crackers and nuts. Guests will eat more at a cocktail party held in late afternoon or early evening, before dinner, than at a party that begins after 8 P.M.

Many cocktail canapes may be frozen on cookie sheets, then transferred to freezer bags and reheated as needed. Warm items should be cooled to room temperature before freezing to prevent the formation of ice crystals. For the best texture and flavor, they should be used within a month.

Thaw phyllo dough overnight in refrigerator, never in the microwave, then place on counter two hours before using. Gather all utensils and ingredients needed before opening package. Open package, quickly unfold dough onto piece of plastic wrap, and completely cover with more plastic wrap and a moist dish towel. Phyllo is a mess to work with if it is exposed too long to air. Peel off sheets as you need them, quickly recovering dough.

The Recipes

Chapter 7
Soups & Salads

The best Christmas present I have ever given is a slim, handmade book of my favorite soup recipes. I packed it in a soup pot and gave it to my niece. For months I imagined the pleasure and surprise of Heidi and her family as they tasted each soup. I knew each one would be among the best soups they had ever had, because I had honed each recipe until it was fit for my personal recipe file.

Over the years, to that clutch of recipes I've added a few and subtracted a couple when vast amounts of cream and butter became passé. But it's safe to say the soup recipes in this chapter have worn well. I'm not tired of any of them, even the mushroom bisque I've been making almost since I learned to cook.

Pair one of the soups with one of the salads and add some crusty bread for a wonderful meal.

Mushroom Bisque

This recipe, based on one from the *New York Times Cookbook* by Craig Claiborne, is a classic. I add a bit more sherry than the original and sometimes substitute half and half for cream, and it's still a knockout—velvety smooth with a deep, rich mushroom flavor that seems to caress the tongue.

1 pound fresh mushrooms,
    cleaned and chopped fine

4 cups chicken broth

1 medium onion, chopped

3 cups milk

6 tablespoons butter

6 tablespoons flour

1 cup whipping cream

Salt, pepper

¼ cup sherry

Place chopped mushrooms, chicken broth and onions in kettle and simmer, covered, for 30 minutes.

Bring milk to a boil in saucepan. In another saucepan, melt butter, add flour and whisk until blended. Add hot milk all at once and whisk vigorously until thick and smooth. Stir in cream.

Stir cream mixture into mushroom broth. Season with salt and pepper. Add sherry and heat through.

Makes 6 to 8 servings.

Coconut-Ginger Squash Soup with Caramelized Apples

Coconut milk, cider and a hint of ginger enhance the flavor of butternut squash in this creamy-smooth soup. A few cubes of caramelized apple are scattered over the top. I created the recipe after enjoying a similar soup in a restaurant.

2½ pounds butternut squash	1½ cups chicken broth
1 cup chopped onions	2 quarter-sized pieces ginger, smashed
3 tablespoons butter	1 (14-ounce) can coconut milk
½ cup dry white wine	1 tablespoon sugar
1½ cups unsweetened apple juice	½ large apple, peeled and cut in ¼-inch cubes

Cut squash in halves and scoop out seeds. Place cut side up on baking sheets. Lightly spritz cut sides with butter spray. Bake in a preheated, 400-degree oven for about 45 minutes or until squash is very soft and beginning to brown. When cool enough to handle, peel and cut into chunks.

While squash cools, sauté onion in 2 tablespoons of the butter in a soup kettle until golden and limp. Add wine and boil until reduced by half. Add juice, chicken broth, ginger and chunks of squash. Cover and simmer for 30 minutes. Transfer half of the mixture to a blender or food processor. Add half the coconut milk and purée until smooth. Repeat with remaining squash mixture and coconut milk. Return to kettle and simmer 10 minutes longer.

While soup simmers, melt remaining 1 tablespoon butter with the sugar in a medium skillet over medium-high heat. Add chopped apple and stir occasionally until butter-sugar mixture begins to turn tawny. Remove from heat.

Ladle soup into bowls and garnish each portion with a teaspoon of caramelized apples.

Makes 8 servings.

Wedding Soup

Vaccaro's Trattoria in Bath makes the definitive version of this soup. In a kitchen session one afternoon, Raphael Vaccaro shared both his recipe and the secret: Adding the egg-cheese mixture in a lump and cooking it until firm, then breaking it apart with a spoon.

3 quarts chicken stock or broth
½ cup finely chopped carrots
½ cup finely chopped celery
½ cup finely chopped onions
2 cups finely chopped endive or escarole
2 cups finely chopped fresh spinach

2 cups tiny meatballs (recipe follows)
4 eggs
2 cups grated Pecorino Romano cheese
1 cup of Acini di Pepe pasta, cooked al dente
Freshly ground black pepper to taste

Measure all ingredients and place them in bowls on the counter, in the order they will be used.

Bring broth to a simmer in a large soup pot. Add carrots, celery, onions, endive and spinach. Add the meatballs. Simmer uncovered for about 30 minutes, until carrots are tender.

In a medium bowl, combine cheese and egg and mix well. Scrape mixture in a lump into the center of the simmering soup. Let simmer for 2 to 3 minutes without stirring. Lift the mass occasionally with a slotted spoon to keep it from sticking to the bottom of the pan. The soup is done when the egg-cheese mixture looks firm. Gently break apart with a spoon.

Remove soup from heat. Stir in the pasta. Season to taste with freshly ground pepper. Serve hot.

Makes 10 to 12 servings.

Tiny Meatballs

1 pound ground veal or chuck
½ pound ground pork
3 eggs
½ teaspoon pepper
Pinch of salt
2 cups Pecorino Romano cheese
½ cup chopped fresh parsley
Seasoned bread crumbs

Gently mix together veal or chuck and pork. Add eggs, pepper, salt, cheese and parsley and mix lightly but well. Gently work in enough seasoned bread crumbs to make a firm mixture. Roll into meat balls the size of grapes.

Place on baking sheets with sides and bake at 350 degrees for 10 to 12 minutes. Meatballs may be cooled, then frozen. Use directly from the freezer.

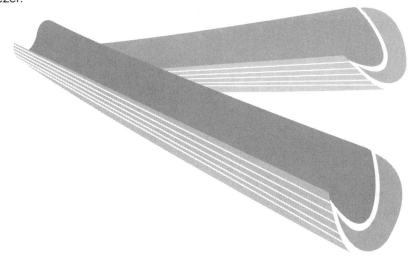

Vichyssoise with Watercress & Grilled Scallops

Vichyssoise is a silk purse made from a sow's ear. Ingredients don't come any humbler than potatoes and leeks. The fancy cold soup was dreamed up by an American chef decades ago. It endures because it flat-out tastes good, especially on a sultry summer evening when a creamy-cold spoonful slides down your throat like a shiver. In my updated version, the cold soup is served with sizzling-hot grilled scallops.

4 tablespoons unsalted butter

1 medium onion, chopped coarse

3 leeks, trimmed, cleaned and chopped (white part only)

4 small to medium Idaho potatoes, peeled and diced

1 quart (32 ounces) chicken broth

1 tablespoon fresh lemon juice

Salt, white pepper

1 bunch watercress

1 cup half-and-half

18 sea scallops

Olive oil

Sprigs of watercress for garnish

Melt butter in a 4-quart kettle over medium heat. Add onion and leeks and slowly sweat until the vegetables are limp but not browned. Add potatoes and cook 5 minutes longer. Add broth, cover and simmer 15 minutes, until potatoes are tender. Let stand until tepid.

In batches, purée the soup thoroughly in a food processor. Stir in lemon juice, salt and pepper.

Return about 1 cup of the soup to the processor, add the watercress and purée until smooth. Stir mixture into the soup. Stir in half-and-half. Chill.

Just before serving, thread scallops on skewers and brush with oil. Grill over a charcoal or gas fire until cooked through but still tender. Remove scallops from skewers and pile three in each of six shallow soup bowls. Place a sprig of watercress on each pile of scallops. At the table, ladle the cold soup around the scallops.

Makes 6 servings.

Jane's Chili

Chili, like happiness, is more a state of mind than an actual thing, and how cooks interpret it is their own business. The way I interpret it is by adding chocolate and brown sugar, but in the true spirit of chili-making, feel free to toss in or leave out whatever you choose.

1½ pounds ground chuck

1 medium onion, chopped

Salt, pepper

2 tablespoons chili powder

1 tablespoon ground cumin

¾ teaspoon ground cinnamon

1 tablespoon oregano

½ teaspoon ground coriander

½ teaspoon (or to taste) cayenne pepper

4 (14.5-ounce) cans whole plum tomatoes

1 (16-ounce) can kidney beans, drained

2 ounces broken Mexican chocolate
  or ¼ cup chocolate chips

1½ tablespoons packed brown sugar

Brown ground beef and onions together in a large pot. Spoon off some of the fat, leaving some in for flavor. Season with salt, pepper, chili powder, cumin, cinnamon, oregano, coriander and cayenne. Cook and stir over medium-high heat for about 2 minutes.

Drain juice from tomatoes into pot. Dice tomatoes and add to pot. Add beans and stir well. Stir in chocolate and brown sugar. Reduce heat and simmer, uncovered, for about 30 minutes, or until flavors are blended.

Makes 8 servings.

Chilled Fresh Tomato Soup

This soup is bursting with the flavor of fresh tomatoes. Roasting concentrates their flavor, and a splash of cream mellows them out.

6 large, ripe tomatoes (about 3½ pounds)

1 medium onion, peeled and halved

2 tablespoons extra-virgin olive oil

2 cloves garlic, minced

1 cup chicken broth

½ teaspoon salt

¼ cup heavy cream

1 cup lightly packed fresh basil leaves

½ cup extra-virgin olive oil

Wash tomatoes and place on a jelly roll pan (a cookie sheet with sides). Add onion halves. Roast uncovered in a preheated, 400-degree oven for 20 to 30 minutes, or until tomato skins have burst and tomatoes begin to slump. Remove from oven and cool slightly.

With a spatula, transfer tomatoes to a wide, shallow bowl to catch their juices. Slip off the tomato skins. With a sharp knife, cut out the stem scars. Reserve juice that has collected from tomatoes. In two batches, purée tomatoes and onion in a food processor until very smooth.

Heat the 2 tablespoons olive oil in a heavy soup kettle. Sauté garlic until softened. Add puréed tomatoes and reserved juice. Stir in broth and salt. Bring to a simmer and simmer 15 minutes, uncovered, to blend and concentrate flavors. Remove from heat and stir in cream. Chill.

In a food processor, purée basil leaves with the ½ cup olive oil until very smooth.

To serve, ladle soup into chilled bowls. Drizzle some basil purée over each and swirl with a spoon.

Makes 6 one cup servings.

Cabbage Soup

When noted Akron cook Helen Davidson shared the recipe for this soup in 1988 at age 85, she said she had cooked every day of her life since her marriage at age 23. After her husband died, she continued cooking and delivering the meals to her children and grandchildren. This hearty soup reflects her Russian-Jewish heritage.

2 medium heads cabbage
1 medium onion
1 pound flanken (beef short ribs)
Water
1 tablespoon salt
1 (28-ounce) can tomato sauce
1 cup brown sugar, or more or less to taste

Wash cabbage and peel onion. Slice cabbage and onion with thin slicing blade of food processor, or thinly slice by hand. Place cabbage, onion, flanken and salt in an 8-quart soup pot. Add enough water to barely cover the meat and vegetables. Simmer, loosely covered, for one hour.

Stir together tomato sauce and brown sugar. Add to soup and continue simmering, barely covered, until meat is tender, about one hour.

Makes 10 to 12 servings.

Fontina-Prosciutto Soup

I want to be one of the ladies who lunch. Instead of cramming my day with work and errands, now and then I would like to sit with a friend in a café at a table by the window, talking of nothing much while watching clock-punchers on their lunch hours dash by. This is what I would eat. The creamy, light cheese broth is punctuated with bits of frizzled prosciutto, and the flavor of roasted garlic permeates every bite.

1 head garlic	6 cups chicken broth
1 tablespoon olive oil	1 bay leaf
3 tablespoons butter	2 cups whipping cream
6 paper-thin slices prosciutto, chopped	1 pound Fontina cheese, shredded
1 cup diced yellow onion	1 tablespoon Marsala wine
¼ cup flour	Salt to taste

Discard any loose outer skin from the head of garlic but don't separate the cloves. With a sharp knife, cut off the tips of the cloves (no more than ⅛-inch), leaving head intact. Place in a small oven-proof bowl or pan and drizzle with olive oil. Bake uncovered at 375 degrees for about 1 hour, until brown and soft. Remove from oven and cool.

Melt 1 tablespoon butter over medium-high heat in a soup pot. Add diced prosciutto and cook and stir over medium-high heat until the edges begin to curl. Remove from the pan with a slotted spoon and set aside.

Melt remaining butter in pot and sauté onion until soft and golden. Sprinkle flour over onions and cook and stir for about 2 minutes. Gradually whisk in broth. Squeeze garlic from papery skins into the broth. Add bay leaf and cream, cover and bring to a boil. Reduce heat and simmer for 30 minutes, until onion is very soft.

In batches, purée soup in a blender. Return to pan. Add cheese a handful at a time, stirring until melted. Stir in Marsala and season to taste with salt. Return prosciutto to soup and simmer a couple of minutes. Ladle into bowls.

Makes about 10 servings.

Vietnamese Chicken Salad

Lunch at a Vietnamese restaurant led me to recreate this boldly flavored salad at home. Fine shreds of Chinese cabbage are heaped on a platter with shredded chicken, fresh mint and cilantro. The salad is sprinkled with chopped nuts and doused with a refreshing lime and rice-vinegar dressing spiked with fish sauce.

½ rotisserie chicken

4 tablespoons fresh lime juice

3 tablespoons rice wine vinegar

1 tablespoon plus 1 teaspoon soy sauce

1 tablespoon Vietnamese fish sauce

1 teaspoon sugar

Pinch crushed red pepper flakes

1 garlic clove, minced

1 small head Napa cabbage, sliced very thin (about 6 cups)

1 tablespoon minced hot pepper, such as serrano

½ cup roughly chopped mint leaves

½ cup cilantro leaves

¼ cup Thai basil leaves, chopped (optional)

½ of a medium red onion, sliced very thin

1½ cups shredded carrots

2 tablespoons minced dry roasted peanuts

Pull the chicken meat into shreds, discarding skin and bones. Place in a bowl and sprinkle with 1 tablespoon lime juice, 1 tablespoon rice vinegar and 1 teaspoon soy sauce. Toss and set aside.

In a small bowl or measuring cup, combine remaining lime juice, vinegar and soy sauce with the fish sauce, sugar, pepper flakes and garlic. Set aside.

In a large bowl, toss together the cabbage, hot pepper, herbs, red onion and carrots. Pour dressing over slaw. Top with shredded chicken and sprinkle with peanuts.

Makes 6 servings.

Fried Green Tomato Salad

When frost threatens, gather the last of the green tomatoes from the garden and use them in this Asian-inspired salad.

Oil

2 ounces rice sticks or 2 cups chow mein noodles

½ cup flour

1 egg beaten with 1 tablespoon water

4 medium green tomatoes, cut in 1-inch cubes (2½ cups)

Salt

2 green onions, with tops, sliced

2 cups shredded iceberg lettuce

4 tablespoons vegetable oil

2 tablespoons rice wine vinegar

1 teaspoon Asian-style sesame oil

2 teaspoons soy sauce

Pour about ½ inch of oil into a wide, heavy skillet and heat until very hot. If using rice sticks, cut with scissors into 4 portions and gently tease apart strands. One portion at a time, fry rice sticks in hot oil until they puff. Turn over and puff again. Drain on paper towels. Set aside. (If using chow mein noodles, no frying is necessary.)

Place flour in a shallow bowl and egg in another bowl. In batches, dip the tomatoes in the beaten egg and dust with flour. Using a small sieve or slotted spoon, transfer the tomato pieces from the flour, shaking off excess, to the hot oil. Fry until golden on all sides. Drain on paper towels. Sprinkle with salt.

When all tomatoes have been fried, combine in a bowl with the green onions and shredded lettuce.

In a small jar, shake together the 4 tablespoons vegetable oil, rice wine vinegar, sesame oil and soy sauce. Pour over salad and toss.

Place rice sticks or chow mein noodles on four salad plates or in four salad bowls. Mound salad on top.

Makes 4 servings.

Jane Snow Cooks

Belgian Endive with Carrots & Walnuts

The various textures, colors and flavors of this tour de force salad makes it a good choice for a special occasion. Ohio Ballet music director David Fisher served it at Christmas dinner parties.

2 heads Belgian endive

½ cup coarse-chopped walnuts

2 tablespoons chopped parsley

4 ounces Roquefort cheese, crumbled

3 to 4 medium carrots, grated

4 tablespoons red wine vinegar

1 teaspoon Dijon mustard

¼ cup walnut oil

1 tablespoon safflower oil

Salt, pepper

Cut root ends from endives and separate into leaves. Wash and pat dry.

Stack up leaves, a few at a time, and cut into thin julienne slivers. Place in a bowl with walnuts, parsley, cheese and grated carrots. Toss gently.

In a jar, combine vinegar, mustard, oils and salt and pepper to taste.

Cover tightly and shake well. Just before serving, drizzle dressing over salad and toss gently.

Makes 4 servings.

Salmon & New Potato Salad

If you think all potatoes are created equal, you've been eating too many frozen hash browns. Miniature new potatoes, plentiful in the spring, have so much flavor they don't require butter. Here, they're showcased in a salad with silky poached salmon.

1 pound small new potatoes	1 teaspoon Dijon mustard
¾ pound salmon fillet	Sea salt
½ cup white wine	Fresh-ground pepper
1 bay leaf	2 tablespoons chopped fresh mint
⅓ cup extra-virgin olive oil	1 tablespoon drained capers
4 tablespoons aged red wine vinegar	6 lettuce leaves
1 clove garlic, smashed	

Steam or boil potatoes until tender, about 15 minutes. Drain and cool.

Meanwhile, place salmon in a saucepan and add wine and bay leaf. Add enough cold water to barely cover fish. Bring to a simmer. Simmer very slowly for 20 minutes. Remove fish from poaching liquid and cool.

While potatoes and fish cool, combine olive oil, vinegar, garlic and mustard in a lidded jar. Shake well. Season to taste with sea salt and pepper.

When potatoes are cool enough to handle but still warm, cut each in half and place in a large bowl. With hands, break fish into bite-size chunks and add to potatoes. Add mint and capers. Drizzle olive oil mixture over all, tossing gently. Chill or cool to room temperature.

Place 2 lettuce leaves on each of three plates. Mound salad on lettuce.

Makes 3 servings.

Panzanella (Tuscan bread salad)

Instead of tossing out stale bread, Italians pair it with diced tomatoes for an addictive salad. Chef Pete Schellenbach provided this terrific recipe for the Italian summer staple. Make it only when you have access to fresh-from-the-vine tomatoes.

2½ cups crusty Italian bread in ½-inch cubes

2 cups cubed ripe tomatoes, in ½-inch dice

½ cup sliced shallots

½ teaspoon minced fresh garlic

2 tablespoons extra-virgin olive oil

2 tablespoons balsamic vinegar

¼ teaspoon salt

Black pepper to taste

½ red onion, sliced thin and separated into rings

½ cup chopped fresh parsley

Bake bread cubes on a cookie sheet at 350 degrees for 10 minutes, or until lightly browned.

In a large bowl, combine tomatoes, shallots, garlic, oil, vinegar, salt and pepper. Let stand at room temperature for about 2 hours or refrigerate overnight. Stir in bread cubes, onion and parsley. Serve immediately.

Makes 4 servings.

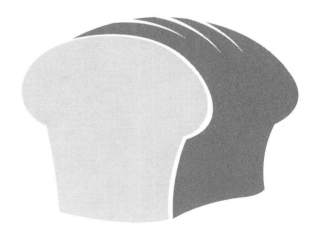

Spinach, Orange & Cashew Salad

Celebrate winter's citrus crop with a fresh-tasting spinach salad studded with orange segments and glossed with a tangy grapefruit-blue cheese dressing. Cashews add flavor and crunch.

¾ cup blue cheese, crumbled (about ¼ pound)
½ cup salad oil
¼ cup grapefruit juice
¼ teaspoon salt
1 cup sour cream
6 cups fresh spinach, washed, drained and broken into bite-sized pieces
6 oranges, peeled and sliced into bite-sized pieces
½ cup cashews

Combine blue cheese, oil, juice and salt in container of blender and blend until smooth. Pour into a jar or bowl and stir in sour cream. Cover and chill at least one hour.

Just before serving, toss together spinach, orange pieces and cashews. Moisten with dressing and toss again.

Makes 6 servings.

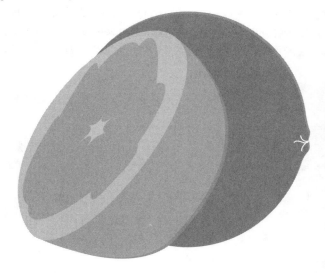

Tips

To the new cook, recipes must appear to be written in code. Exactly what are fresh bread crumbs, anyway?

Some translations:

Bake at 350 degrees: unless otherwise noted, always preheat the oven.

Minced parsley: just the leaves, never the bitter stems.

Flour: when there are no qualifiers, it means all-purpose.

Brown sugar: the measurement is based on packing the sugar into the cup or spoon.

Grated vs. shredded: to grate, use a food processor or the fine holes of a grater. To shred, use the large holes.

Make a well: in baking, it means making a bowl-like indentation in the dry ingredients.

Deglaze pan: adding liquid to a pan in which something has been cooked and stirring up the brown bits that have stuck to the bottom.

Stiff peaks: when egg whites have been beaten to the stiff-peak stage, they will be glossy and stand in a slightly drooping peak when the beater is removed. If the whipped whites are dull and have begun to break into clumps, they are over-beaten. To rescue them, add another egg white.

Scald: bringing a liquid, usually milk, to just below the boiling point.

Fresh bread crumbs: made from fresh bread, pulverized in a food processor or blender and used while soft.

The Recipes

Chapter 8
Vegetables

So you can't stand broccoli and you never touch squash? That's like saying you don't like music when all you've heard in your life is one tune by Ozzy Osbourne.

What you probably don't like is plain broccoli boiled within an inch of its life and slapped on a dinner plate next to the meatloaf. And plain, unseasoned, whipped squash, the kind that is frozen into blocks for adults and piped into tiny jars for infants.

No, you don't have to eat your vegetables. Not when they taste like that. There's more than one way to cook a vegetable, though, and dozens of ways to dress them up. A squeeze of lemon juice and a few minutes shaved off the cooking time may be all that stands between love and hate.

We're not talking about major kitchen time here. I once saw a recipe for brussels sprouts that called for shredding the sprouts (figure that one out), sautéing them with garlic and prosciutto, simmering them in cream and wine, and baking them with Parmesan cheese. Most people don't spend that much time making a complete Sunday dinner.

With a few exceptions, the recipes I like are quick fixes that can turn a plain vegetable into a luscious one in a matter of minutes. I culled the best from my cache to share with you.

Sautéed Radishes

Radishes become an entirely different vegetable when rolled around in a hot skillet. When heat is applied for about three or four minutes, the peppery punch mellows but the crispness remains.

1 bunch radishes
1 tablespoon butter
Pinch of coarse sea salt
3 tablespoons marsala wine
⅛ teaspoon dried tarragon

Trim radishes, leaving whole if small and cutting into halves or fourths if large. The pieces should be about ¾-inch across. You should have about 1¾ cups.

Heat a large skillet over medium-high heat. Do not use a coated nonstick skillet. Add butter and when it melts and begins to sizzle, add radishes and season with sea salt. Cook, shaking pan occasionally, for 2 minutes or until radishes just begin to take on color.

Add wine and tarragon and shake the pan to glaze the radishes. When the wine has boiled away, remove from heat and give the radishes another sprinkle of sea salt.

Makes 4 servings

Jane Snow Cooks

Bourbon-Mashed Sweet Potatoes

Chef David Russo makes these irresistible sweet potatoes. They're voluptuously rich but not cloying, with flavor notes of cinnamon, nutmeg and bourbon.

8 medium sweet potatoes, about 4 pounds	½ teaspoon cinnamon
2 teaspoons salt	¼ teaspoon nutmeg
1 tablespoon granulated sugar	¼ cup cream
1 tablespoon packed brown sugar	4 tablespoons butter
½ teaspoon salt	¼ cup Steen's Cane Syrup (or white corn syrup)
¼ teaspoon white pepper	½ cup bourbon

Peel sweet potatoes and cut into quarters. Cut each quarter in half again. Place in a pot and cover with cold water. Add the 2 teaspoons salt and granulated sugar. Bring to boil, reduce heat and simmer for about 15 minutes or until very tender. Potatoes should mash easily when pressed with a fork.

Drain potatoes and return to pan over very low heat. Return to burner until all moisture has evaporated, about 2 minutes. Remove from heat. Rice or mash until very smooth.

Stir in brown sugar. Combine the ½ teaspoon salt, pepper, cinnamon and nutmeg in a small bowl; stir into potatoes.

Place cream and butter in a saucepan. Heat until butter melts. Stir into potatoes. Stir in the corn syrup and bourbon.

Makes 8 to 10 servings.

Note: Potatoes may be made up to a day in advance and reheated in a saucepan with an additional ¼ cup cream.

Maque Choux

Maque choux is a humble cajun bayou dish of sautéed corn enriched with whatever the cook has on hand. I like to throw in some hot sausage, onions and red bell pepper, and reduce some chicken stock to its flavor essence while the corn is cooking. The upshot is a side dish that will steal the show.

6 ounces hot sausage, bulk or cured and cut into cubes

3 tablespoons butter

1 tablespoon oil

1 cup minced onion

⅓ cup diced red bell pepper

¼ teaspoon (or to taste) cayenne pepper

Kernels from 7 ears corn

½ cup chicken broth

Salt, pepper

Brown sausage in a large skillet. Remove from pan and set aside. In same skillet with sausage grease, heat 2 tablespoons of the butter and the oil over medium heat. Add onion, bell pepper and cayenne and sauté until softened.

Add corn to skillet and cook and stir for 3 minutes. Add broth, increase heat to high and boil until broth has evaporated. Stir in remaining 1 table-spoon butter. Season to taste with salt and pepper.

Makes 4 large servings.

Sweet Potatoes with Cider & Almonds

Chef Scot Jones brought this dish to a pre-Thanksgiving chef's dinner at my house. It's not overly sweet, as most sweet potato casseroles are, and has a depth of flavor achieved by simmering the potatoes with a cinnamon stick and cider before puréeing with almonds and dotting with butter.

4 pounds sweet potatoes (about 8 medium)
2½ cups apple cider
1 cinnamon stick (2 inches)
½ cup packed dark brown sugar
8 tablespoons butter
½ cup sliced almonds

Peel potatoes and cut into 1-inch cubes. In a large saucepan, combine potatoes, cider, cinnamon, brown sugar and 6 tablespoons of the butter. Bring to a boil, partially cover and simmer, stirring occasionally, until the potatoes are very tender, about 20 minutes.

Cool mixture slightly. Remove cinnamon stick. Purée potatoes and liquid in batches in a food processor with half the almonds. Combine batches of puréed potatoes and stir until smooth.

Transfer to a buttered, 2-quart baking dish. Dot surface with the remaining 2 tablespoons butter, cut into small pieces. Sprinkle remaining almonds on top. Bake at 350 degrees for 30 minutes.

Makes 8 servings.

Julienned Squash with Walnut Butter

If you know a squash hater, serve them this and watch them eat their words. Virginia chef Marcel Desaulniers once made a dish similar to this at a food conference in California. I liked it so much that, back home, I experimented to come up with this knockoff version.

6 walnut halves
4 tablespoons butter, softened
½ medium butternut squash
1 medium acorn squash
Salt, pepper

Place walnut halves in a pie pan and toast at 300 degrees for 15 to 20 minutes. Cool and chop fine. Mix with softened butter.

Peel squash with a sharp potato peeler and scoop out seeds with a spoon. With a knife or julienne blade of a food processor, cut flesh into strips about 2 inches long and ⅛-inch wide.

Melt walnut butter in a large skillet. Add squash strips and sauté over medium-high heat just until tender, about 7 minutes. Season with salt and pepper.

Makes 4 servings.

French Potato Salad with Garlic & Mint

The French use a vinaigrette instead of mayonnaise to dress potato salad. My favorite version is dressed up further with lots of garlic and mint.

12 small new potatoes

¼ cup extra-virgin olive oil

½ teaspoon balsamic vinegar

4 large cloves garlic, minced

2 heaping tablespoons minced fresh mint leaves

1 teaspoon coarse sea salt or to taste

Freshly ground black pepper

Pierce potatoes with a fork and roast in a microwave or conventional oven until tender. Quarter potatoes while hot and toss with remaining ingredients. Serve at room temperature.

Makes 4 servings.

Cuban Black Beans & Rice

From Miami via a Tallmadge resident comes this reliably good recipe for the Cuban national dish. I've made it dozens of times and have never been disappointed. The beans may be served on their own or as a side dish with grilled pork or beef.

½ pound dried black beans

1½ quarts water

2 large onions, chopped

1 green pepper, chopped

4 cloves garlic, chopped

½ cup olive oil

1 tablespoon salt

1 ounce bacon

¼ pound ham bone

2 tablespoons oregano

3 bay leaves

½ cup vinegar

Cooked white rice

Chopped onion for garnish (optional)

Wash and sort beans. Cover with water by 2 inches and soak overnight. Or bring to a boil, remove from heat and let stand 2 hours.

Drain beans. In a skillet, fry onion, green pepper and garlic in olive oil until tender. Add to beans along with the 1½ quarts water, salt, bacon, ham bone, oregano and bay leaves. Cook over low heat until beans are tender and of a thick consistency, about 2 to 3 hours. Add vinegar a few minutes before serving. Serve over rice, topped with raw chopped onion.

Garlic Mashed Potatoes

Many restaurants serve these potatoes, and many cookbooks offer recipes. Most call for roasting the garlic, which takes about an hour in the oven. A simpler method is to simmer peeled garlic cloves in the milk or cream, which not only makes the cloves mellow and sweet, but flavors the cream.

2 pounds small red potatoes
¾ cup cream
5 large cloves garlic, peeled
4 tablespoons unsalted butter
Salt, pepper

Scrub potatoes but do not peel. Place in a kettle and cover with water. Bring to a boil and simmer for about 20 to 30 minutes, until potatoes are tender.

Meanwhile, place cream and peeled garlic in a small pan. Simmer for about 30 minutes, until garlic is soft and sweet.

Drain potatoes and return to pan. Place over low heat until remaining moisture evaporates. Remove from heat and add garlic and butter. Begin mashing by hand, adding warm cream a little at a time until desired texture is reached. Season with salt and pepper.

Makes 4 to 6 servings.

Summer Mediterranean Gratin

If summer was a food, it would taste exactly like this. Baking instead of frying the sliced eggplant cuts down on the oil, and sprinkling the minced herb and bread crumb mixture between each layer infuses the entire casserole with flavor. On a dining trip to San Francisco, this dish from chef Gary Danko lingered in memory long after much fancier fare was forgotten.

1½ pounds eggplant, peeled and sliced ½-inch thick

½ cup olive oil, or as needed

Salt, pepper to taste

1½ pounds zucchini, sliced into ¼-inch rounds

3 medium onions, minced fine

1½ pounds fennel bulbs, sliced ¼-inch thick

½ cup fresh bread crumbs

1 cup grated Parmesan cheese

4 tablespoons chopped green onion tops or chives

4 tablespoons chopped fresh basil

4 tablespoons chopped fresh chervil

4 tablespoons chopped Italian parsley

2 tablespoons chopped fresh thyme

1½ pounds large tomatoes, cored, sliced ¼-inch thick

Place eggplant slices on a thick baking sheet. Brush both sides with a thin coating of olive oil. Bake at 450 degrees for 10 minutes, until golden brown on the bottom. Turn and bake about 5 minutes longer. Cool. Season lightly with salt and pepper.

Heat a large sauté pan over medium-high heat. Add 3 tablespoons olive oil. Add zucchini slices (in batches if necessary), turn heat to high and sauté 4 minutes. Remove from pan and salt lightly.

In same pan, place 3 tablespoons of olive oil; add onion and sauté 4 minutes. Add fennel and cook over low heat, stirring occasionally, until tender, about 30 minutes. Season with salt and pepper. Let cool.

Combine bread crumbs, cheese, green onions, chopped herbs and salt and pepper to taste.

To assemble, lightly brush a 10-by-16-inch gratin dish (or other shallow casserole) with oil. Spread half of the onion-fennel mixture in bottom and, in succession, cover with one layer of sliced tomatoes, one layer of zucchini and one layer of eggplant, seasoning each layer with the bread crumb mixture.

Repeat, ending with a layer of tomatoes. Top with remaining bread crumb mixture. Drizzle with a little olive oil.

Bake at 400 degrees for 30 to 40 minutes, or until hot and slightly brown on top. Let stand 30 minutes before cutting into squares. Serve warm or at room temperature.

Makes 6 to 8 servings as a main dish, 8 to 10 as a side dish.

Roger's Grilled Smashed Potatoes

Small, cooked redskin potatoes are gently flattened, basted with a spicy vinaigrette, and grilled. Chef Roger Thomas' smashed potatoes were the hit of a chefs' potluck picnic in 1995.

12 small (golf-ball size) redskin potatoes

2 tablespoons kosher salt

1 bay leaf

3 tablespoons white vinegar

3 cloves garlic, minced

3 tablespoons ground cumin

1 tablespoon sugar

1 teaspoon cayenne pepper

6 tablespoons extra-virgin olive oil

Scrub potatoes under running water. Put in a large saucepan with 1 tablespoon of the salt and bay leaf. Cover with cold water. Bring to a gentle boil over medium heat and simmer until soft but not falling apart (8 to 10 minutes). Chill 3 hours or overnight.

Combine remaining ingredients in a small bowl and stir well. Smash potatoes between the palms of your hands to ½-inch thickness. Place on grill 2 to 3 inches above hot coals. Baste tops with vinegar mixture. Grill 3 to 5 minutes, until nicely browned. Turn potatoes over and baste again, grilling until underside is crisp and brown. Remove to a plate and baste again. Serve warm.

Makes 6 servings.

Winter Vegetable Hash

This recipe for vegetable hash is modeled on memories of the gutsy versions I've enjoyed in restaurants. Winter root vegetables are finely diced and roasted until soft and almost caramelized. Slice the vegetables and then stack to dice them more quickly.

1 small celery root, ¾ pound (2¾ cups diced)

1 large turnip, ½ pound (1¾ cup diced)

1 pound parsnips (3½ cups diced)

2 medium carrots (1¼ cups diced)

1 medium potato (1 cup diced)

2 cloves minced garlic

½ cup chopped onion

3 tablespoons olive oil

Sea salt

1 teaspoon dried thyme

1 teaspoon chopped fresh rosemary

¼ cup white wine vinegar

With a good-quality vegetable peeler, peel vegetables. Cut into ¼- to ½-inch cubes. Combine in a large bowl with garlic and onion and mix well.

Heat olive oil in a large, deep frying pan over medium-high heat. Add diced vegetables and sauté for 15 minutes, turning occasionally with a spatula. Stir in salt, thyme and rosemary. Add vinegar and toss with the vegetables, turning rapidly with a spatula until vinegar has evaporated.

Place pan of vegetables in an oven preheated to 350 degrees. Roast for 45 minutes, or until vegetables are soft and top begins to brown.

Makes 6 to 8 servings.

Roasted Beets with Raspberry Vinegar

If the only beets you've tasted came from a can, fresh beets will be a revelation. Roasting brings out the sweetness while retaining their delicate, earthy flavor. Raspberry vinegar is the perfect foil.

6 medium beets, about 2 inches in diameter (about 1 pound)

2 tablespoons raspberry vinegar

1 tablespoon olive oil

1 tablespoon snipped fresh chives

Sea salt

With a sharp knife, trim the leafy stems to within a half-inch of the beet tops. Do not trim the root end. Gently wash the beets and place in a baking pan. Add ½ inch of hot water. Cover tightly with foil. Bake at 350 degrees for 1 to 1½ hours, until the beets can be pierced easily with a fork. Uncover and cool.

Trim off the top and root ends in a sink. Slip off the skins under cool running water. Over the sink, cut the beets into batons about ½ inch wide and as long as each beet.

Place beets in a bowl. In a small bowl, whisk together the vinegar, oil and chives. Drizzle over the beets, tossing gently. Season to taste with sea salt. Chill. Toss again just before serving.

Makes 4 to 6 servings.

Tips

If you hate to can, simply freeze your excess summer tomatoes. The easiest way is to place whole tomatoes in zipper-lock bags and freeze. Use in soups and sauces. The skin will come right off and float as the tomatoes cook.

Or make tomato purée by simmering peeled, seeded and chopped tomatoes until thick. When cool, pour into freezer containers, leaving 1-inch head space. Herbs can lose flavor or become bitter when frozen, so season the purée after thawing.

Peel tomatoes by submersing in boiling water for about 30 seconds, then plunging into cold water. The skin slips right off. De-seed tomatoes by cutting in half horizontally, then squeezing as you would an orange.

If you've ever tried to peel a raw butternut squash, you have faced adversity. The knife blade goes in, the tough skin resists, and you barely miss slicing off your finger.

The only easy way to peel tough-skinned winter squash is with a very sharp potato peeler. Buy a new one if yours is old and dull—it's well worth the modest price.

The Recipes

Chapter 9
Entrées

E ach recipe in this book brings back memories of meals with friends and conversations with readers. For me the memories have been sweet and occasionally funny. I laughed when I came across the recipe for Stir-Fried Rice Noodles with Beef and Broccoli in this chapter. My husband and I had just gotten engaged and celebrated with a trip to New York City. He's a slim guy with an enormous capacity for food. He was on a Chinese noodle kick that weekend, and between meals he would stop at one or two noodle shops for a "snack" of a wad of noodles the size of my head. I was astounded. When I returned home, I began hungering for all the noodles I had been too full to even try, and created the stir-fried noodle recipe.

The Flank Steak Picnic Sandwich recipe reminds me of a sunny summer day in June when I phoned three chefs and asked them to meet me in two hours at Blossom Music Center with picnic. I wanted to see what kind of alfresco meal the pros could pull together when under the same time constraints as the rest of us, who usually grab carry out on the way to the concert. No fair using kitchen staff, I told them.

Moe Schneider of Moe's Restaurant in Cuyahoga Falls showed up with a big round loaf of bread stuffed with strips of steak, arugula, artichokes, roasted red peppers, goat cheese and brined black olives. She plopped the sandwich on a blanket on the lawn and cut it into wedges. It tasted as good as it looked.

Some of the recipes in this chapter were developed in response to a trend. When chicken pot pies started showing up in restaurants both fast and fancy, I tasted them all and then created a clone of the soul-warming KFC Chicken Pot Pie.

Other recipes came about after a stroll thorough a supermarket to see what was on special. When beef prices climbed a few years ago, I loaded my cart with bargain cuts, then simmered beef shanks with cumin and coriander for Southwestern Beef Shanks. Think of it as a Mexican version of osso buco.

However each recipe started, they have one thing in common: I love them all. I hope you do, too.

Yankee Carolina Pulled Pork Barbecue

Let's just get all the Texans riled up and be done with it: The best barbecue in the world is the pork barbecue produced in the back hills and piney woods of the Carolinas. The succulent pulled pork (pulled as in shredded, not sliced) is served in a pile or heaped on a bun and topped with coleslaw. Making this ambrosial barbecue at home was a quest of mine for years. I finally got it down pat.

1 pork butt roast, 4 pounds	1 tablespoon salt
1 quart charcoal briquettes	1 tablespoon paprika
4 small chunks of hickory wood	1 teaspoon dry mustard
2 tablespoons black pepper	½ teaspoon cayenne pepper

Bring roast to room temperature while preparing the fire. For the fire, pile the charcoal on one side of a covered grill and light. Soak the hickory chips in water. When the coals are white around the edges, combine pepper, salt, paprika, mustard and cayenne and rub it evenly over the roast.

Scatter the hickory chunks over the pile of coals (do not spread). Place grid on grill. Place roast on grid, on the side away from the coals. Cover and adjust top vents so they are one-quarter open. Bottom vents should remain fully open.

Cook pork for 4 hours, opening lid as infrequently as possible. It should not be necessary to add more coals.

Remove roast from grill and tightly seal in a double thickness of foil. Bake at 300 degrees for 3 hours, until an instant-read thermometer registers 210 degrees.

Unwrap roast and place on a cutting board. Shred the meat with a fork. Lightly dress with barbecue sauce (preferably Carolina vinegar-based), or pass the sauce at the table. Pile the meat on hamburger buns and top with coleslaw.

Makes 8 servings.

Pecan-Crusted Pork Tenderloin with Honey-Ginger Sauce

Pork tenderloin is almost as lean as boneless, skinless chicken breasts. The cut is incredibly versatile, too. The mild flavor takes to everything from fruit relishes to Asian spices. This Asian-inspired treatment is a great company dish because all of the preparation can be done in advance and the final roasting takes just thirty minutes.

1 pork tenderloin, about 1 pound	2 tablespoons soy sauce
2 tablespoons Dijon-style mustard	2 tablespoons orange juice
½ cup chopped pecans	1 clove garlic, minced
2 tablespoons honey	1 quarter-size piece of fresh ginger, minced

Trim any fat from the tenderloin. Fold 2 inches or so of the tail toward the fatter part of the tenderloin and tie in place with string, so that the piece of meat is all one thickness.

Brush the meat with 1 tablespoon of the mustard. Roll in the chopped pecans, coating evenly on all sides. Place on a cookie sheet and roast at 375 degrees for about 30 minutes, until the meat is barely pink in the center.

Meanwhile, combine remaining tablespoon of mustard in a lidded jar with the honey, soy sauce, orange juice, garlic and ginger. Shake well.

To serve, remove the string and cut the meat into ½-inch slices. Spoon some sauce onto each plate and arrange the slices over the sauce.

Makes 3 to 4 servings.

White Pizza

Pizza bliss is a chewy crust topped with a creamy garlic-Parmesan sauce, chopped fresh tomato and crisp bacon. Top it off with plenty of melted mozzarella for a pizza you'll dream about. The crust may be purchased but the white sauce must be homemade.

3 tablespoons butter	1 tablespoon butter
1 clove garlic, minced	1 12-inch pizza shell
2 tablespoons flour	4 slices bacon, cooked crisp
⅔ cup milk	1 large tomato, diced
2 tablespoons fresh-grated Parmesan	1½ cups finely shredded mozzarella
Salt, pepper	¼ cup fresh-grated Parmesan
1 cup sliced mushrooms	

In a saucepan, melt the 3 tablespoons butter and sauté garlic briefly. Add flour and whisk over medium heat until flour is golden. Whisk in the milk. Cook and stir over medium heat until sauce thickens. Remove from heat and add the 2 tablespoons Parmesan, salt and pepper.

In a skillet, sauté mushrooms in remaining 1 tablespoon butter until cooked through. Drain.

Spread sauce on pizza shell (or over dough, if using fresh dough). Scatter mushrooms evenly over sauce. Crumble bacon and scatter over pizza. Top with diced tomato. Combine mozzarella and remaining ¼ cup Parmesan and sprinkle over pizza. Bake at 450 degrees for 10 minutes for a prebaked crust, or 425 degrees for 15 to 20 minutes for a fresh-dough crust.

Makes 3 to 4 servings.

Cincinnati Chili

This recipe supposedly came from the Cincinnati-based Skyline Chili chain years ago, according to a local resident who shared it. Those in the know order it by the number. One-way is plain chili, two-way is chili over spaghetti, three-way is with cheese, four-way is with chopped onions and five-way is all of the above plus beans.

2 pounds ground beef

5 cups water

1 teaspoon cinnamon

½ teaspoon cumin

2 large onions, chopped

2 teaspoons Worcestershire sauce

1 clove garlic

1 tablespoon chili powder

½ teaspoon black pepper

1 tablespoon salt

¼ to ½ tablespoon cayenne pepper

1 (6-ounce) can tomato paste

½ teaspoon vinegar

½ tablespoon ground allspice

3 bay leaves

Cooked spaghetti, shredded Cheddar cheese, chopped onions, beans

Crumble beef into water in a large pot. Add remaining ingredients except spaghetti and toppings. Bring to a boil, cover and simmer for 3 hours.

Remove garlic and bay leaves. Drain off any broth that you don't need, or leave as it. Serve over spaghetti with cheese, onions and beans to add at the table.

Chiles Rellenos with Goat Cheese & Mango Salsa

Poblano peppers are great for stuffing. They're dark green and resemble small, pointed bell peppers. They range in length from about 3 to 4 inches, and are considered medium hot. The heat of any chili pepper can be reduced by careful cleaning. Remove every speck of ribs and seeds, the parts that hold the heat. In this recipe, the poblanos are roasted before stuffing, which both sweetens the flavor and makes them more tender.

12 poblano chili peppers	1 tablespoon ground cumin
2 tablespoons vegetable oil	Salt, pepper
2 cloves garlic, minced	2 small tomatoes, seeded and chopped
1 medium onion, chopped	1 cup golden raisins
¾ pound ground turkey	½ cup stuffed green olives, sliced
1 jalapeño, seeded and minced	4 ounces goat cheese

Roast whole peppers over a stove burner or on a charcoal grill until charred on all sides. Place in a paper bag, close top and let steam for about 5 minutes. Remove from bag and peel off charred skin under running water. Set aside.

Heat oil in a large skillet. Sauté garlic and onion until softened. Add turkey and jalapeño and sauté until turkey no longer is pink.

Stir in cumin, salt, pepper and tomatoes. Cook until any moisture has evaporated. Stir in raisins and olives. Remove from heat and cool slightly. Crumble goat cheese into mixture and stir well.

Make a lengthwise slit on one side of each pepper and carefully remove seeds. Stuff peppers with meat mixture, mounding stuffing above the slit. Place in a lightly greased baking pan and bake at 350 degrees for 10 to 15 minutes, until cheese is melted and tops begin to turn golden.

Serve 2 peppers per person for an entrée or 1 for an appetizer. Top with mango salsa.

Makes 6 to 12 servings.

Mango Salsa

1 ripe mango
1 green onion, sliced
2 tablespoons chopped fresh cilantro
2 teaspoons olive oil
Juice of ½ lime

Remove the mango seed by slicing thick slabs off the sides of the mango. When all the flesh has been sliced away, peel the skin off the slabs with a sharp knife. Cut the flesh into ½-inch cubes. Place in a bowl with remaining ingredients and toss.

Tandoori Chicken

Tandoori chicken is a spicy dish that is usually baked in a brick oven. Wooster engineer Mohammed Moinuddin adapted the traditional Indian recipe for a regular home oven. In his recipe, chicken pieces are slathered with a mixture of sour cream, ground almonds and spices before baking. The flavor is spectacular.

2 tablespoon oil

1 large onion, chopped

2 cloves garlic

1 cup chopped cilantro leaves

1 teaspoon garam masala or tandoori masala, purchased or homemade (recipe follows)

1 teaspoon paprika

½ teaspoon turmeric

1 teaspoon grated fresh ginger

1 cup sour cream (or very thick yogurt)

½ teaspoon salt

2 ounces slivered almonds, ground fine

6 pounds chicken pieces

Heat oil in a large skillet. Cook onions until they are transparent and begin to brown. Scrape into a food processor with the garlic and cilantro leaves. Purée until almost smooth. Add spices, ginger, sour cream and salt and pulse to mix. Pour into a large bowl and stir in almonds.

Remove skin and all fat from chicken. Place chicken in sour cream mixture, coating on all sides. Cover and refrigerate several hours or overnight.

Remove chicken from marinade, allowing marinade to cling to meat. Arrange on a baking sheet with sides. Spoon more of the marinade over the chicken. Bake uncovered at 375 degrees for 1 hour, or until tender. If chicken begins to release too much juice, raise the heat to 400 degrees until juices evaporate.

Makes six to eight servings.

Garam Masala

½ cup cumin seeds

2 tablespoon coriander seeds

4 cinnamon sticks, each 2 inches long

10 to 12 green cardamom pods, slightly crushed

4 to 5 black cardamom pods, slightly crushed

10 whole cloves

½ nutmeg, broken

1 tablespoon black peppercorns

4 whole star anise

5 bay leaves

Place all spices in a dry, nonstick skillet over very low heat. Cook until spices begin to give off a fragrance, shaking pan occasionally. Cool slightly, then grind finely in a coffee mill or electric blender. Store in an airtight bottle.

Thai Salmon with Rice Sticks

Salmon takes to the grill like no other fish. It's a medium-fat fish, so it doesn't dry out as quickly as leaner species. The fillets are thick, so they don't fall apart. And there's something about the marriage of salmon and hickory that elevates the flavor—which already is great—to the sublime. I like the interplay of hot salmon and cold sauce, and this Thai coconut-lime sauce is one of my favorites.

1 teaspoon minced ginger	Vegetable oil
1 large clove garlic, minced	2 tablespoons olive oil
¼ cup soy sauce	4 salmon fillets, each about 2 inches wide
½ cup coconut milk	2 small pieces of hickory, soaked in water
¼ cup lime juice	4 green onions, green part only, sliced
1 ounce (about) thin rice sticks	

In a small saucepan, combine ginger, garlic, soy sauce, coconut milk and lime juice. Bring to a boil and cook over medium-high heat for 2 minutes to blend flavors. Transfer to a measuring cup, cover and chill.

With scissors, snip off 4 pieces of rice sticks, each about half the size of your hand. Gently tease apart the strands into a fan shape. Heat about a half-inch of oil in a wide skillet until very hot. Drop in 1 mass of rice sticks and when the noodles puff, turn with a spatula. When the noodles puff again, remove and drain on paper towels. Noodles should not brown. Continue with remaining rice sticks.

Build a medium-hot charcoal fire. Oil the flesh side only of the salmon fillets with the olive oil. When coals ash over, place hickory on the coals. Place fillets on grill, skin-side down. Close lid and cook 10 minutes, or until salmon is just cooked through. Turning is not necessary. With a spatula, remove fillets from grill, leaving skin behind.

Place a mass of noodles on one side of each of four dinner plates. Spoon sauce on the other side. Rest salmon fillets against the noodles and over the sauce. Sprinkle with chopped green onions.

Makes 4 servings.

Oven-Barbecued Short Ribs

These beef short ribs take three hours to cook, but after the initial sauté, they're hassle-free. Just sit back, relax and sniff occasionally as your home fills with the warm aroma of simmering meat and sauce. Judge Ed Bayer shared the recipe for an "In the Kitchen" column.

4 pounds beef short ribs, trimmed of all visible fat

3 tablespoons vegetable oil

1½ cups minced onion

2 cloves garlic, minced

1 (15-ounce) can tomato purée

⅓ cup fresh lemon juice

3 tablespoons Worcestershire sauce

2 tablespoons Dijon-style mustard

2 tablespoons dark brown sugar

2 tablespoons red wine vinegar

1 tablespoon ground cumin

1 teaspoon salt

¾ teaspoon cayenne pepper

Pat ribs dry with paper towels. Brown ribs in oil in skillet. Remove ribs and sauté onions and garlic in same skillet. Add remaining ingredients (except ribs) to skillet and stir, scraping up brown bits. Simmer for 5 minutes.

Place ribs in 9-by-13-inch baking dish. Pour sauce over ribs. Bake, covered with foil, at 325 degrees for at least 3 hours, turning every 30 minutes or so. Sauce can be made in advance and stored in the refrigerator.

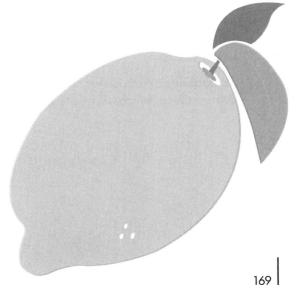

Stuffed Cabbage Rolls

For years, the star of Beth El congregation's Jewish food festival was Ann Sacks' cabbage rolls. She made more than 1,000 of them annually for the Akron event. The Russian-style cabbage rolls are mellow with prunes and raisins and sweetened with brown sugar.

2 medium-large heads cabbage, about 5 pounds

2 pounds ground chuck

1 tablespoon salt

½ teaspoon pepper

1 large onion, grated

2 cloves garlic, crushed

3 tablespoons Worcestershire sauce

3 tablespoons ketchup

1 tablespoon homemade chicken fat, softened (optional)

1 whole large egg

¼ cup ice water

¾ cup raw Minute Rice, cooked 1 minute in salted, boiling water

Core cabbage and blanch for 5 minutes in boiling water. Remove from water and plunge into cold water. Carefully remove leaves from heads, separating leaves into piles of small, medium and large leaves. With a sharp paring knife, trim the thick center vein of each leaf so that the vein does not protrude above the surface of the leaf.

Combine remaining ingredients, mixing very lightly. Place a well-rounded tablespoon (about the size of an egg) of the mixture on the end of a large cabbage leaf (use less mixture for a medium or small leaf). Roll once and tuck in one side. Continue to roll and tuck in other side, forming a neat bundle. Repeat with remaining mixture and cabbage leaves. Don't pack leaves too tightly.

Set cabbage rolls aside for layering in pot and prepare the following uncooked sauce, which will be used between cabbage layers.

Uncooked Sauce

1 large (28-ounce) can whole tomatoes, diced. Drain and reserve juice.

½ cup cold water

1½ large onions, grated

¾ cup fresh lemon juice

3 large cloves garlic, crushed

¾ cup dark brown sugar

¼ teaspoon pepper

1¼ teaspoons salt

1 piece (¾-inch) fresh, medium-hot pepper, diced

¾ cup dark raisins

15 pitted prunes

Finely chopped parsley for garnish

Combine reserved tomato juice and water and put in bottom of large, wide pot to prevent burning the cabbage rolls. Combine all remaining sauce ingredients in a bowl.

Place largest cabbage rolls in a layer on top of juice-water mixture in bottom of pot. Top with one-third of sauce mixture. Add layer of medium-size rolled cabbages. Top with more sauce. Add layer of small cabbage rolls and top with remaining sauce mixture.

Cover and simmer gently for 2 hours, tasting frequently and adjusting seasonings to taste. Add more lemon juice, brown sugar and salt, if necessary. Serve in soup bowls, garnished with chopped parsley.

Makes about 36 cabbage rolls.

Barbecued Mojo Turkey with Chipotle-Citrus Sauce

Brining—soaking in salt water—is an essential part of barbecuing a turkey. Brining poultry almost guarantees that the meat will be creamy, silky and juicy. Here, I add citrus and garlic for a Cuban-inspired flavor. I tested this recipe on a covered kettle grill with indirect heat (i.e., not directly over the coals) so that the exterior wouldn't burn before the meat cooked through. Don't bother using a gas grill; you might as well roast it in the oven.

1 gallon water	1 lime
1 pound table salt	Butter or olive oil
¼ cup sugar	1 handful hickory or mesquite wood chips, soaked for 30 to 60 minutes in water
2 cups orange juice	
2 cups lime juice	4 cloves garlic
1 bulb garlic	1 cup mayonnaise
½ cup olive oil	½ canned chipotle chili in adobo sauce (or to taste)
½ cup chopped cilantro	
10 whole peppercorns	Grated rind of ½ lime, ½ orange
1 whole turkey (any size)	Juice of ½ lime, ½ orange
1 orange	2 tablespoons chopped cilantro leaves

In a large insulated cooler, combine the water, salt, sugar, orange and lime juices. Separate the bulb of garlic into cloves, peel and chop. Add to the cooler. Add the oil, cilantro and peppercorns. Stir to dissolve the salt.

Place turkey in cooler, add plenty of ice and close the lid. Let stand overnight or up to 2 days, turning turkey occasionally and replenishing ice often.

Grate the zest and squeeze the juice from half of each lemon and lime, for use in the sauce. When ready to grill, remove the turkey from the brine and pat dry. Place both halves of the orange and lime in the turkey cavity. Place an oblong foil pan in the bottom of the grill. Pile at least 40 charcoal briquettes along each long side of the pan, outside the pan. Light the coals.

When the fire is hot and the coals are ashed over, scatter some of the wood chips over the coals and immediately place the turkey in the center of the cooking grid, over the pan. If parts of the turkey extend beyond the pan, shield them with foil. Grease the turkey with butter or oil. Close the lid, making sure the vents in the lid are fully open and the vents in the bottom of the grill are unplugged. Do not use a grill that does not have both top and bottom vents.

Try not to lift lid too often, which will lower the temperature, but check every 45 minutes and replenish briquettes as needed, adding about 10 each time along with additional wood chips. To add briquettes and wood, you will have to lift the turkey from the grill, so have a platter handy.

Cook the turkey for 2½ to 3 hours for a 12-pound turkey and up to 5 hours for a 20-pound turkey. Use an instant-read thermometer. Stick it in the thickest part of the thigh, not touching the bone. The turkey is done when the thermometer registers 175 to 180 degrees. Let turkey rest 15 minutes before carving into slices and drizzling with sauce.

To make the sauce, drop garlic cloves through the feed tube of a food processor while the motor is running. Stop processor, add remaining ingredients, replace lid and process until smooth. If necessary, add more juice to produce a sauce the consistency of thin pancake batter. Chill.

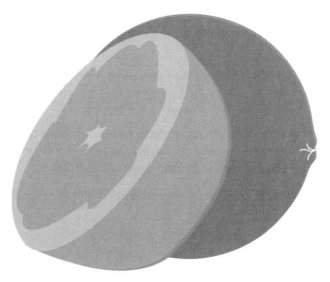

Stir-Fried Rice Noodles with Beef & Broccoli

Like many of my recipes, this one gives you a lot of flavor for very little work. The sauce may be made in big batches and stored for weeks in a jar in the refrigerator.

7 ounces ¼-inch-wide rice noodles	2 tablespoons vegetable oil
3 cups broccoli florets	1½ tablespoons minced fresh ginger
6 tablespoons soy sauce	4 green onions, cut in 1-inch pieces
2 tablespoons dry sherry	½ pound top sirloin, sliced very thin
1 tablespoon Asian chile bean sauce	¼ teaspoon red pepper flakes
1 teaspoon sugar	½ cup lightly packed fresh cilantro leaves
1 tablespoon minced garlic	

Soak noodles in hot water to cover for 15 minutes. Drain. Meanwhile, cook broccoli in hot water until barely tender. Drain. While broccoli cooks and noodles soak, combine soy sauce, sherry, chile bean sauce, sugar and ½ teaspoon of the garlic in a small bowl or measuring cup; stir well.

Heat a large skillet over high heat until very hot. Add oil. When the oil begins to shimmer, add remaining 1 tablespoon garlic, ginger and green onions. Stir-fry for 1 minute. Add beef and continue to stir-fry until most of the redness is gone, about 2 minutes.

Sprinkle with red pepper flakes and give the mixture a big stir. Add broccoli and noodles and stir to coat with oil. Add sauce and stir and fold until noodles are tender and sauce is absorbed.

Mound on two plates and sprinkle with cilantro.

Makes 2 servings.

Flank Steak Picnic Sandwich

Moe Schneider of Moe's Restaurant in Cuyahoga Falls created this hearty but sophisticated sandwich for an article about picnics at Blossom Music Center.

1 hollowed-out loaf of crusty bread, about 10 inches in diameter

1 pound flank, top sirloin or flat iron steak

Salt, pepper

2 tablespoons balsamic vinegar

2 handfuls baby arugula that has been tossed with balsamic vinegar, olive oil, salt and pepper

1 cup drained, chopped artichoke hearts

2 whole roasted red peppers, slivered

½ cup crumbled goat cheese

1 cup pitted Kalamata olives, chopped in food processor or by hand with 2 cloves garlic

To hollow out the bread, cut loaf in half horizontally and remove some of the interior with your fingers, leaving a 1-inch-thick shell of bread and crust.

Season steak on both sides with salt and pepper. Grill or broil for 3 minutes. Turn over and splash with 1 tablespoon balsamic vinegar. Grill for 3 minutes longer or until medium-rare. Turn and splash with remaining 1 tablespoon vinegar. Let stand while assembling remaining ingredients, then slice steak across the grain into ¼-inch slices.

Arrange sliced steak in bottom half of bread loaf. Top with arugula mixture, then artichoke hearts, roasted peppers, goat cheese and olive mixture. Replace top of loaf. Wrap tightly in plastic wrap and chill. Unwrap and cut into 6 wedges before leaving for picnic. Wrap tightly and transport in a cooler.

Makes 6 servings.

Ham with Gingersnaps

Former Akron City Club chef Ed Valente dreamed up this homespun recipe one Christmas when we asked five chefs to make hams for a homeless shelter. The ham is simmered in ginger ale, which flavors the meat, and then baked with a gingersnap crust.

1 fully cooked ham, 9 pounds or larger
2 liters Vernor's ginger ale
½ pound gingersnaps, crushed
½ cup brown sugar
⅓ cup molasses
½ bottle Heinz 57 Sauce
¼ to ½ cup maraschino cherry juice

Place ham in a tall kettle and cover with ginger ale. Bring to a boil, reduce heat and simmer for 1¼ hours. Remove ham from liquid and cool.

Combine remaining ingredients in a bowl to make a paste. Brush some of the mixture over ham. Bake uncovered at 300 degrees for 45 minutes. Continue baking about 2 to 2½ hours longer, until ham is heated through, brushing with mixture as needed. Serve warm.

Jane Snow Cooks

Curried Chicken with Cashews

Former Blossom Music Center manager Al De Zon, an enthusiastic and eclectic cook, provided the recipe for this boldly flavored chicken curry. Ground cashews thicken the sauce and give it a subtly nutty flavor.

3 tablespoons ghee or oil

2 large onions, minced

3 cloves garlic, minced

2 teaspoons grated fresh ginger

3 tablespoons regular curry powder

1 teaspoon cayenne pepper

2 teaspoons salt

3 large ripe tomatoes, peeled and chopped

2 tablespoons chopped fresh coriander or mint

3½ pounds chicken parts

2 teaspoons garam masala

½ cup plain yogurt

4 ounces raw cashews, ground

In a large, deep frying pan, heat ghee and gently sauté onion, garlic and ginger until soft and golden. Add curry powder and cayenne and stir for 1 minute. Add salt, tomatoes and coriander and cook until mixture has formed a sauce.

Add chicken pieces to pan, turning to coat with sauce. Cover tightly and simmer over low heat for 45 minutes, or until chicken is tender, stirring occasionally.

Stir in garam masala and yogurt and simmer, uncovered, for 5 minutes.

Stir in cashews and heat through. Garnish with more chopped coriander, if desired. Serve with rice.

Cajun Chicken Pizza

This lush pizza can be made in just twenty minutes, yet tastes like it came from a gourmet pizza restaurant.

1 12-inch pizza shell

2 tablespoons olive oil

1 pound boneless, skinless chicken breasts

1½ tablespoons Cajun seasoning (any commercial brand)

1 cup shredded mozzarella cheese

1 cup shredded fontina cheese

1 (16-ounce) can whole tomatoes, drained

¼ cup grated Parmesan cheese

Place pizza shell on a baking sheet. Spread 1 tablespoon olive oil over crust.

Cut chicken into strips about ¼-inch wide and 2 inches long. Heat remaining 2 tablespoons oil in a large skillet. Stir-fry chicken over high heat for 2 minutes. Add Cajun seasoning and stir-fry 2 minutes longer, or just until chicken is cooked through. Do not overcook, or chicken will be tough. Set aside.

In a bowl, mix together mozzarella and fontina cheeses. Spread over pizza crust. With hands, break up tomatoes into chunks; drain well. Arrange over cheese. Top with chicken strips, then sprinkle with Parmesan.

Bake according to directions that come with crust (10 minutes at 450 degrees for Boboli crust).

Makes 2 to 3 servings.

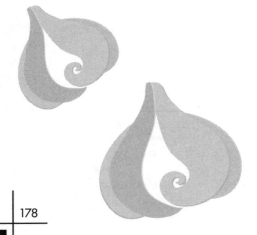

Stromboli Chop Bread

A crazy quilt of bread dough, meats and cheeses are chopped together on a cutting board, piled onto a baking sheet and fused into a round, flavorful loaf in the oven. Pack a wedge in your lunch box, serve it with soup for supper, or take a loaf to a pot luck. Vary the ingredients to create your own flavors.

1 loaf frozen white bread dough	½ cup drained, mild banana pepper rings
¼ pound sliced salami	1 teaspoon oregano
1 cup (4 ounces) shredded mozzarella	3 cloves minced garlic

On a cutting board lightly sprayed with vegetable oil spray, thaw dough at room temperature for 2 hours, or until thawed. Pat into a 10-inch circle on cutting board. Cover with a cloth and let rise in a warm place for about 1 hour, or in an air-conditioned house for 2 hours, or until doubled in bulk.

Or dough may be thawed and risen overnight in the refrigerator, in a bowl lightly coated with vegetable oil spray. Pat dough into a 10-inch circle on a cutting board and continue with recipe.

Cut stack of salami slices into fourths. Place in a bowl with remaining ingredients and toss well, making sure salami pieces are separated. Pile onto dough.

Draw dough up around mixture. With a large, sharp knife, slice bundle about five or six times across, then five or six times in the other direction. With knife, gently mix by lifting dough and salami mixture from bottom and piling on top. The dough pieces should be about 2 inches square.

With a spatula, gently mound mixture on a lightly greased baking sheet, reshaping into a circle and making sure most of the filling touches the dough.

Bake at 350 degrees for about 30 minutes, or until puffy and brown. Remove from oven and let stand 10 minutes before removing from baking sheet. Serve warm or cold. To reheat, bake at 350 degrees for 5 to 10 minutes, or until heated through.

Southwestern Beef Shanks

Southwestern seasonings turn a bargain cut of beef into a glorious, slow-simmered meal. This is my spiced-up version of the Italian classic, osso buco. Inch-thick beef shanks are available at most grocery stores.

1 teaspoon ground cumin

2 teaspoons pure chili powder

1 teaspoon salt

¼ teaspoon dried oregano

1 teaspoon ground coriander

½ teaspoon garlic powder

4 beef shanks, about 1 inch thick

3 tablespoons olive oil

½ cup carrots, diced into ¼-inch pieces

1 cup chopped onion

2 cloves garlic, minced

½ cup halved cherry or grape tomatoes

1 (2.5-ounce) can sliced ripe olives

1 (4-ounce) can diced green chilies

Beef broth (about ½ to ¾ cup)

In a custard cup, stir together cumin, chili powder, salt, oregano, coriander and garlic powder. With kitchen shears, snip the band of fat circling each shank. Rub meat on both sides with spice mixture.

Heat 2 tablespoons of the olive oil over medium-high heat in a skillet large enough to hold meat in a single layer. When oil is very hot, brown beef on both sides. Remove from heat and transfer beef to a plate.

Add remaining olive oil to skillet and return to heat. Add carrots, onion and garlic and sauté for 3 to 5 minutes, until limp but not brown.

Return meat to skillet, pushing vegetables aside and spooning them on top of meat. Scatter tomatoes, olives and chilies over meat. Add enough beef broth to come almost halfway up sides of beef shanks. Cover and simmer for about 1½ hours, until tender.

Makes 4 servings.

Jane Snow Cooks

Almost KFC Chicken Pot Pie

A comforting chicken pot pie can be on the table in a hurry with the help of frozen puff pastry and rotisserie chicken. This recipe produces a dead ringer for the luscious pot pies sold by the fried-chicken chain.

1 rotisserie chicken

1 sheet Pepperidge Farm frozen puff pastry (half of a 17 ¼-ounces box)

6 medium potatoes (about 1½ pounds)

1½ cups sliced carrots

1 cup frozen peas

Salt, pepper

2 cans (10¾ ounces each) Campbell's condensed cream of chicken soup

2 soup cans milk

1½ teaspoons sugar

Remove skin from chicken and shred meat into bite-sized chunks. Measure out 4 cups and set aside, reserving any remaining chicken for another use.

Remove puff pastry sheet from box and thaw at room temperature. Meanwhile, scrub potatoes and cut into ½-inch cubes (peeling is not necessary). Place in a large pot. Add carrots. Barely cover with hot water. Cover, bring to a boil and simmer until vegetables are just tender, about 10 minutes. Place frozen peas in a strainer. Pour potatoes and carrots over the peas in the strainer and drain. Season with salt and pepper.

In same pot, combine soup and milk, stirring until smooth. Heat to a simmer. Stir in sugar. Add shredded chicken and vegetables and simmer until warmed through.

Unfold pastry sheet and roll out on a lightly floured board to a rectangle slightly larger than a 9-by-12-inch pan. Pour hot filling into pan. Moisten edges of pastry and place over filling, moistened edges down. Fold edges over rim of pan and press to seal.

Bake at 400 degrees for 20 minutes, or until pastry is golden brown.

Makes 6 generous portions

The Recipes

Chapter 10
Desserts

I was lucky enough to have a mother who served dessert for dinner twice a year. When blackberries were in season, we would spend a day in the woods picking a bucket full, and that evening after dinner there would be warm blackberry cobbler. Period. We would scoop the steaming cobbler into bowls and add a splash of cold milk.

The second dessert supper would be in the autumn, when we would visit an apple orchard and buy a bushel to turn into candied apples for Halloween. But first, Mom would spend the afternoon making flaky apple turnovers that would be ours. Forgoing vegetables for second and third helpings of dessert felt wickedly good.

I have not only kept the family cobbler tradition going, but have branched out to cakes, puddings, ice cream, sorbets, scones, pastries, soufflés and fruit soups. If it has sugar in it, I've probably not only made it but hauled it to work to be photographed.

The dessert recipes in this chapter are some of my current favorites. They range from easy to semi-complicated, from cookies to cream puffs, from chocolate to cranberry. I tried to include recipes that would appeal to a broad range of tastes and even threw in a fudge recipe because Northeast Ohio goes crazy for fudge on holidays.

I believe that if everybody ate more ice cream the planet would be a gentler place. If we made more time for piña colada cream puffs and peach meringue pie, we would smile more and fight less. While dessert cannot remedy all ills, it may help us endure them.

Gingerbread Biscotti

Gingerbread is hard for me to resist, so I was thrilled when a reader shared her recipe for gingerbread biscotti. The cookies aren't as rock-hard as most biscotti, and the combination of ginger and chocolate is heavenly.

1 cup blanched whole almonds
¾ cup sugar
¼ pound (1 stick) butter
½ cup dark molasses
3 eggs
3 cups flour
1½ teaspoons baking powder

1 tablespoon cinnamon
1 teaspoon ground nutmeg
1½ teaspoons powdered ginger
½ teaspoon ground cloves
½ teaspoon ground allspice
½ pound white or dark chocolate coating

Place almonds in an 8- or 9-inch-square pan. Bake at 350 degrees until golden, 10 to 15 minutes. Cool, chop coarse and set aside.

In a large bowl of an electric mixer, beat sugar, butter and molasses until smooth. Add eggs one at a time, beating well after each addition.

In another bowl, stir together flour, baking powder, spices and almonds. Add to egg mixture, stirring to blend.

On 2 greased, 12-by-15-inch baking sheets, use well-floured hands to pat dough into 4 flat loaves, spacing them evenly on the sheets. Each loaf should be about ½-inch thick, 2 inches wide and the length of the baking sheet.

Bake at 350 degrees for 25 minutes, or until browned at the edges and springy to the touch (rotate position of pans halfway through baking). Cool on baking sheets for 3 to 4 minutes only, then cut into ½-inch slices on the diagonal.

Arrange biscotti on baking sheets, close together with a cut side down. Return to oven and bake at 350 degrees for 15 to 18 minutes, until cookies are brown, switching position of pans halfway through. Transfer cookies to racks and cool completely.

Melt coating in a saucepan. Dip half of each cookie in the chocolate coating. Dry on racks, then store in an airtight container. Cookies may be stored at room temperature up to 1 month, or frozen.

Makes about 50 biscotti.

Pecan Cream Cheese Pie

If you know how to use a mixer, you can make this pie. I've taken it to many pot-lucks because it can be made quickly, yet tastes like it came from the dessert cart of a fancy restaurant. The pie is rich, so cut it into small pieces.

Filling

1 package (8 ounces) cream cheese, softened

⅓ cup sugar

¼ teaspoon salt

1 teaspoon vanilla extract

1 egg

1 9-inch unbaked pie shell

Topping

1¼ cups chopped pecans

3 eggs, beaten

¼ cup sugar

1 cup light corn syrup

1 teaspoon vanilla extract

For the filling: Beat cream cheese and sugar with an electric mixer until fluffy. Add salt, vanilla and egg, beating just until egg is incorporated. Pour into pie shell.

For the topping: Sprinkle pecans over cream cheese mixture in pie shell. In a bowl, beat together eggs, sugar, corn syrup and vanilla. Pour over pecans.

Bake at 375 degrees for 35 to 40 minutes, until center is firm. Cool.

Rum-Raisin Fudge

If you're not eating fudge at Christmas time, get outta here. Go on back to Texas or New Jersey or some other gawd-forsaken fudge-less state. In the Akron area, holiday candy equals fudge, period. Amateur fudge-maker Sheri Tarshis shared this prized recipe one December.

2 cups sugar

½ cup sour cream

¼ cup (4 tablespoons) margarine

12 ounces white chocolate, chopped

1 (7 ounces) jar marshmallow creme

½ cup golden raisins

1 teaspoon rum extract

Combine sugar, sour cream and margarine in a saucepan. Bring to a rolling boil over medium heat, stirring constantly. Boil for 5 minutes, stirring constantly, until mixture registers 236 degrees on a candy thermometer.

Remove pan from heat and stir in white chocolate, marshmallow, raisins and rum extract. Beat vigorously for several minutes, until fudge begins to thicken. Pour into a greased, 8-inch-square pan. Cool, then cut into squares.

Peach-Pecan Upside-Down Cake

The pecans halves toast to a sweet crunchiness and the peach slices form a gorgeous pinwheel pattern on this fresh variation of upside-down cake. Make this cake when peaches are in season, and use fruit that is slightly firm rather than dead-ripe.

1 stick (8 tablespoons) butter
¾ cup packed brown sugar
2 to 3 peaches, peeled and cut in ½-inch-thick slices
15 pecan halves
1 box (about 18 ounces) spice cake mix

In a 10- to 11-inch cast-iron skillet melt butter and brown sugar over low heat, stirring until smooth. Remove from heat. Arrange peach slices and pecans in a pretty pattern over the sugar mixture. Set aside.

Prepare cake mix according to package directions. Pour about two-thirds of the batter over the fruit in the skillet, filling the pan no more than three-fourths full.

Bake at 350 degrees for 30 to 35 minutes, or until cake seems solid and bounces back when lightly pressed. Immediately invert onto a serving platter. Cool to lukewarm before cutting.

Makes 8 to 10 servings.

Black Raspberry Cream Pie

Black raspberries grow in profusion along Ohio's roads and the boundaries of farmers' fields in the summer. Here's a dandy way to use them, reminiscent of the raspberry cream pies at Gardner's Pies in Barberton.

¾ cup sugar

¼ cup flour

1 cup evaporated milk

¾ cup skim milk

1 cup black raspberries, washed and drained

1 8-inch pie shell

Stir together sugar and flour in a 2-quart saucepan. Stir in evaporated and skim milk. Cook over medium heat, stirring, until it just reaches the boiling point. Remove from heat.

Spread berries in the bottom of the pie shell. Pour hot milk mixture over berries. Bake at 350 degrees for 30 to 35 minutes, until the crust is golden and the filling is set. Cool before cutting.

Ultimate Pumpkin Pie

I always figured that if God had wanted us to make pumpkin pies from scratch she wouldn't have created pumpkin purée in cans. But curiosity got the better of me and now I'm hooked. When you start with a pumpkin, the flavor is a delicate cross between canned pumpkin and whipped yams, with a texture more like crème brûlée than baked custard.

1 or 2 small pumpkins, about 2 or 3 pounds total

Pastry for a 1-crust, 10-inch pie

1 egg beaten with 1 tablespoon water

¾ cup packed dark brown sugar

¼ cup granulated sugar

1 tablespoon flour

1 tablespoon molasses or dark corn syrup

1½ teaspoons ground cinnamon

1 teaspoon ground ginger

¼ teaspoon fresh-grated nutmeg

¼ teaspoon ground cloves

¼ teaspoon salt

3 eggs

1¾ cups cream

2 tablespoons brandy or rum

Place whole pumpkins in a large kettle and cover with water. Bring to a boil, and boil, covered, for about 30 to 45 minutes, depending on size. When done, the pumpkins can be pierced easily with a fork. Drain and cool.

Remove stems, peel off skin and with a sharp knife, cut strings and seeds away from flesh. Use a sharp teaspoon to finish removing guts. Cut flesh into 1-inch cubes and purée in batches in a food processor.

Transfer purée to a sieve lined with cheesecloth and let drain for 30 minutes. Draw cheesecloth around purée and gently squeeze out more liquid. Measure out 2 cups.

Roll out pastry and fit into a 9½- or 10-inch pie pan. Crimp edges. Brush edges with egg-water mixture. If desired, roll out scraps and cut into the shapes of leaves. Brush with egg-water mixture and bake the leaves on a cookie sheet at 375 degrees for 10 to 15 minutes, until golden.

In a large bowl, combine sugars, flour, molasses, cinnamon, ginger, nutmeg, cloves and salt. Stir in the 2 cups pumpkin purée.

In another bowl combine eggs, cream and brandy. Slowly pour into the pumpkin mixture, whisking until smooth. Pour into pie shell.

Bake on the middle oven rack at 375 degrees for 40 to 50 minutes, or until a knife inserted in the filling comes out clean. When wiggled, the filling should still move slightly in the center. Cool. Decorate with pastry leaves, if desired.

Makes 1 pie.

Summer Fruit Tart

A French-style tart is a great way to showcase ripe summer fruit. In this recipe, the fruit is arranged over a thin layer of coconut pastry cream, made easy by beating thickeners into the eggs before adding the hot milk. Don't be intimidated – the whole process takes about forty-five minutes from start to finish, and the tart is a knockout.

Pâte sucrée (recipe follows)
Coconut pastry cream (recipe follows)
1½ peaches, peeled and sliced
½ cup blueberries
1½ kiwi fruit, peeled, halved lengthwise, cut into ¼-inch slices

½ of a mango, peeled and sliced
½ cup blackberries
¼ cup raspberries (Or any combination of soft, ripe fruits)
2 tablespoons currant jelly, melted

Prepare and bake a 10- to 11-inch pâte sucrée tart crust using a tart pan with removable sides. Cool. Prepare and cool the pastry cream.

Spread the pastry cream in the crust. Arrange fruit over the pastry cream in concentric circles. Brush the fruit with melted jelly. Chill. Remove tart pan sides just before serving.

The pastry cream and crust may be made a day in advance. The tart may be assembled several hours before serving.

Makes 12 servings.

Pâte Sucrée

1½ cups flour
¼ cup sugar
¼ teaspoon salt

9 tablespoons butter, chilled
1 egg, beaten
1 to 2 tablespoons ice water

Combine flour, sugar and salt in the bowl of a food processor. Cut butter into grape-sized chunks and drop into the feed tube while the processor is running. Work quickly so the dough does not overmix.

With the motor running, pour the beaten egg into the feed tube. Stop motor. Add 1 tablespoon water and pulse briefly. If necessary, add second tablespoon of water until dough clumps together into a ball.

Wrap dough in plastic wrap and chill for at least ½ hour to allow gluten to relax. Roll out dough on a floured cloth to a circle 1½ inches wider in diameter than the tart pan.

Gently ease dough into bottom and up sides of tart pan. Do not stretch the dough. Patch any torn places. Gently press dough into sides of tart pan. With a rolling pin, roll off the excess dough hanging over the tart pan sides.

Prick dough all over with a fork. Cover with foil, patting dough into corners and crevices. Fill with about 1 cup of raw beans or rice. Bake at 400 degrees for 15 minutes.

Remove foil and beans or rice from pan. Reduce heat to 350 degrees and bake tart shell 10 to 15 minutes longer, until edges start to turn golden. Remove from oven and cool to room temperature.

Coconut Pastry Cream

1 cup milk

⅓ cup cream

¼ cup sweetened flaked coconut

3 egg yolks

⅓ cup sugar

2 tablespoons flour

1 tablespoon cornstarch

½ teaspoon vanilla extract

Combine milk, cream and coconut in a saucepan. Bring to a simmer. Meanwhile, beat together egg yolks and sugar with a mixer until light and lemon-colored. Beat in flour and cornstarch a little at a time.

Add the milk mixture in a thin stream, beating constantly. Return to pan and stir over low heat until mixture thickens, about 3 to 5 minutes. Remove from heat and stir in vanilla. Chill.

Green Tomato Pie

A local chef shared her grandmother's recipe for this homespun pie. Make it when the tomato vines are threatening to take over the garden.

4 cups peeled, thin-sliced green tomatoes	¼ teaspoon salt
1¼ cups sugar	5 tablespoons flour
½ teaspoon cinnamon	2 tablespoons fresh lemon juice
½ teaspoon nutmeg	Pastry for a 2 crust pie

To peel tomatoes, plunge into boiling water for 2 to 3 minutes, then drain and slip off the skins. Slice tomatoes and place in a large bowl; set aside.

Blend together sugar, cinnamon, nutmeg, salt and flour. Sprinkle tomatoes with lemon juice, then toss with the sugar mixture.

Place tomato mixture in a pastry-lined 9-inch pie pan. Cover with top pastry and cut steam vents in pastry. Crimp and seal edges. Bake at 425 degrees for 50 to 60 minutes, until tomatoes are soft and crust is lightly browned.

Hungarian Apricot Meringue Diamonds

Layered apricot-nut diamonds topped with meringue are much-loved by local cooks, and this version is one of the best. It was shared by a Munroe Falls baker, whose grandmother brought the heirloom recipe to this country from Hungary decades ago. The delicate cookies are filled with apricot preserves and ground nuts and topped with browned meringue. They're a bit of work, but worth it.

⅔ cup lukewarm milk

1 cake yeast

1¾ cup plus 1 teaspoon sugar

3 cups all-purpose flour

½ pound butter or margarine

6 egg yolks, beaten

1 jar (2 pounds) apricot preserves

4 cups ground nuts

6 egg whites

Dissolve yeast and 1 teaspoon sugar in the warm milk. Mix together flour and butter as for pie dough. Combine beaten egg yolks with yeast mixture and add to flour-butter mixture. Mix well. Shape into a ball and divide into 3 portions.

On a floured surface, roll out one portion of dough until it is large enough to fit an 11-by-18-inch cookie sheet. Place on sheet and spread with one-half of the preserves. Combine nuts with 1 cup of the sugar. Sprinkle one-third of the nut mixture over the preserves.

Roll out second piece of dough to fit the cookie sheet. Place on top of first layer of dough, jam and nuts. Spread with remaining preserves and another one-third of the nut mixture. Roll out remaining dough and place over layers on cookie sheet. Cover and let rise in a warm place for 1 hour.

Bake at 375 for 30 minutes. Just before done, beat egg whites until soft peaks form. Gradually add remaining ¾ cup sugar, beating until egg whites are stiff and glossy. Remove pastry from oven and top with meringue. Sprinkle remaining nut mixture over meringue. Return to oven and bake 5 minutes more, or until lightly browned. Cool, then cut into diamond shapes.

Makes about 5 dozen.

Coconut-Pecan Bread Pudding

Picture thick slabs of bread pudding loaded with pecans and shredded coconut and dripping with a buttery bourbon sauce. Geoffrey Hewitt of Akron shared the recipe along with a hunk still warm from the oven. The contrast in soft and crunchy textures is killer.

1 long loaf French bread	1 tablespoon dry sherry
1 cup chopped pecans	2 tablespoons vanilla extract
4 cups milk	1 cup raisins
2 cups sugar	1 cup shredded coconut
½ cup (1 stick) butter, melted	1 teaspoon cinnamon
3 eggs	½ teaspoon nutmeg

Tear the bread into pieces of various sizes and let air-dry for 3 days. Spread chopped pecans on a baking sheet and toast at 350 degrees for 15 minutes. Combine all ingredients except bread and mix well. Add bread and stir well, using your hands to thoroughly mix the ingredients. The mixture should be quite moist but not soupy. Add more milk if it appears to be too dry.

Pour into a greased, 9-by-13-inch baking pan. Bake at 350 degrees for 1 hour and 15 minutes. Serve warm with bourbon sauce.

Makes 10 servings.

Bourbon Sauce

½ cup (1 stick) butter
1½ cups confectioners' sugar
1 egg yolk, lightly beaten
½ cup bourbon or other liquor

Stir butter and sugar over low heat until sugar is dissolved. Remove from heat and stir in egg yolk. Stir in bourbon gradually. Heat until warm but not boiling. Spoon over individual portions of bread pudding.

Makes about 1½ cups.

Blueberry Gelato

For a week in the summer of 1987 I tested and discarded recipe after recipe for ice cream. None compared to the creamy-rich gelato I tasted in Italy until I stumbled on this unassuming recipe from cookbook author Giulliano Bugialli. I tried it, tweaked it and put it in my personal recipe file. Even after a week in the freezer, the gelato remains silky-smooth. Other fruits may be substituted for the blueberries to vary the flavor.

  4 egg yolks
  6 tablespoons granulated sugar
  ½ cup milk
  1 teaspoon vanilla extract
  ¾ pound blueberries
  1 teaspoon confectioners' sugar
  2 cups whipping cream

Place yolks and granulated sugar in a bowl and beat until the eggs are thick and lemon-colored. Slowly beat in milk. Scrape into top part of a double boiler. Place over boiling water. Stir constantly over medium-low heat with a wooden spoon until the custard thickens. It should heavily coat a spoon. Do not allow custard to boil.

Remove from heat and stir in vanilla. Continue stirring for 2 minutes. Transfer to bowl to cool.

When custard is cold, add fruit. Stir in confectioners' sugar and whipping cream. Freeze in an ice cream maker according to manufacturer's directions.

Makes about 1 quart.

Flourless Chocolate Cake with Bourbon

This is the best flourless chocolate cake I've tasted, and I've sampled a few. The recipe was shared in a "Recipe Roundup" column.

½ cup raisins

½ cup bourbon or cognac

1 cup pecan halves

4 ounces semisweet chocolate

8 ounces bittersweet chocolate

3 sticks (24 tablespoons) unsalted butter

⅓ cup sugar

2 tablespoons cornstarch

6 eggs

Sifted confectioners' sugar

Soak raisins in bourbon for at least 2 hours. Toast nuts on a cookie sheet at 400 degrees for about 10 minutes, until they begin to brown. Reserve 8 nuts for decoration and coarsely chop the rest.

Line a 12-inch round cake pan with buttered parchment. Reduce oven temperature to 350 degrees. Drain liquor from raisins, reserving raisins and liquor.

Melt chocolate with butter and sugar in a heavy saucepan over low heat. Stir until smooth. Scrape into a large bowl.

In a small bowl, combine the liquor and cornstarch. In a medium bowl, combine the eggs, raisins, bourbon-cornstarch mixture and chopped pecans. Add to the chocolate mixture and beat vigorously until mixture begins to thicken. Pour into prepared cake pan. Bake at 350 degrees for 18 to 20 minutes. Cool to lukewarm. Cut in small slivers to serve.

Piña Colada Cream Puffs

In this tropical take on classic cream puffs, I simplified the filling by using pudding mix and added crushed pineapple, flaked coconut and a dash of rum extract. The dough isn't difficult to make, although beating it will give your triceps a workout.

Filling

1 box (2¾ ounces) vanilla pudding mix (not instant)

2 cups whole milk

½ cup flaked, sweetened coconut

1 (8-ounce) can crushed pineapple, very well drained

¼ teaspoon rum extract

Topping

1 cup confectioner's sugar

1 tablespoon water

6 tablespoons flaked, sweetened coconut

Dough

1 cup water

6 tablespoons butter

1 teaspoon salt

½ teaspoon sugar

¾ cup flour

4 eggs

For the filling: Cook pudding according to package directions, using the 2 cups milk. Scrape into a bowl, cover surface directly with plastic wrap and chill until cool. When cool, fold in coconut and pineapple. Stir in rum extract. Chill until ready for use.

For the dough: In a heavy saucepan, heat water, butter, salt and sugar over medium-low heat until butter melts. Remove from heat and stir in flour all at once, beating with a wooden spoon until smooth. Return to heat briefly, stirring until dough leaves sides of pan and forms a smooth mass.

Remove from heat and make a well in the center of the mass. Add an egg and beat with a wooden spoon until the paste has absorbed all of the liquid, and reformed into a smooth mass. Repeat with remaining eggs.

On a lightly buttered baking sheet, measure out ¼ cup of dough and place in a mound. Repeat five times. With a tablespoon, top each mound of dough with smaller blobs of dough.

Bake at 425 degrees for 20 to 25 minutes, until puffed and golden brown. Remove from oven and with a sharp knife, make a small slit in each puff. Return to oven for 10 minutes. Cool on wire racks.

When ready to fill, cut cream puffs in half horizontally and pull out any moist dough inside. Fill with pudding mixture. Replace tops.

For the topping: Combine confectioner's sugar and water and beat until smooth. Drizzle icing over tops of puffs. Sprinkle with coconut. Serve immediately.

Makes 6.

Cranberry Crumb Tart

A cranberry tart heaped high with a sweet streusel topping became a holiday favorite in many homes after San Francisco pastry chef Jim Dodge shared the recipe in a Hudson cooking class. It is a show-stopper, and it tastes as good as it looks.

1 9- or 10-inch tart shell (recipe follows)
6 cups fresh cranberries, washed, any stems removed
2½ cups sugar
½ teaspoon kosher salt
12 tablespoons unsalted butter
1¼ cups bread flour

Make and cool tart shell. For filling, combine cranberries with ¾ cup of the sugar and the salt and toss to coat berries. Spoon into prebaked tart shell, mounding slightly in center.

For crumb topping: Cut butter into 1-inch cubes. Using paddle attachment on electric stand mixer, mix butter, flour and remaining 1¾ cups sugar at medium-low speed just until mixture forms large clumps that crumble when pinched. Do not overmix. Spoon crumb topping over berries. Do not press topping into fruit.

(If your mixer doesn't have a paddle attachment, cut butter into flour and sugar with a pastry blender).

Bake tart at 375 degrees until topping is golden brown and fruit bubbles around edges, about 40 minutes. Serve at room temperature.

Jane Snow Cooks

Tart Shell

¼ cup (4 tablespoons) unsalted butter, cold

1 teaspoon sugar

⅛ teaspoon kosher salt

¾ cup flour

3 tablespoons whipping cream

Cut butter into 1-inch cubes. Place in mixer bowl with sugar, kosher salt and flour. Using paddle attachment, blend at low speed with an electric mixer until mixture resembles coarse meal. Add whipping cream and mix until dough comes together.

On slightly floured surface roll dough into 13-inch circle. Fold into quarters and lift into 10- or 9-inch tart pan (a pan with straight rather than angled sides). Unfold circle carefully and settle into pan, being sure dough reaches into corners. Gently press dough against sides of pan.

Fold overlapping dough into pan just to where sides and bottom meet, to form double-thick sides. Gently press dough against sides of pan, being careful not to press against bottom. (If too thin where sides meet bottom, dough will split during baking.) Trim off extra dough by running rolling pin around top edge. Chill until firm, about 20 minutes.

Line tart shell with heavy foil, covering edges as well as bottom. With fork pierce holes all over bottom of shell, through both foil and dough. Hold fork straight down so tines do not tear large holes in dough. Bake at 400 degrees until inside of shell looks pale but no longer raw (lift foil and look), 15 to 20 minutes. Remove foil and continue baking until shell is golden brown and has pulled away from sides of pan, about 15 minutes more. Cool.

White Chocolate-Sour Cherry Rice Pudding

A humble dessert goes haute with the addition of white chocolate and dried sour cherries.

1 cup long-grain rice	3 cups milk
5 egg yolks	1 teaspoon vanilla extract
½ cup sugar	1 cup white chocolate chips
¼ cup flour	½ cup dried sour cherries or cranberries
1 cup cream	

Cook rice according to package directions until just barely done. Grains should still be slightly firm. Pour into a strainer and drain completely.

Meanwhile, beat egg yolks and sugar with an electric mixer until thick and pale yellow. Beat in flour. Heat cream and milk until almost simmering. Beat into egg mixture in a slow stream.

Pour custard into a saucepan. Bring to a boil, whisking lazily to prevent custard from scorching. After the first bubbles appear, boil 3 minutes longer, whisking constantly, until thick.

Remove from heat and stir in vanilla, rice, chocolate and dried cherries. Let stand 2 minutes, until chocolate melts. Stir again. Spoon into dessert bowls or parfait glasses. Garnish with whipped cream, if desired. Serve warm.

Makes 6 servings.

Fresh Peach Sundaes with Caramel-Peanut Sauce

Biting into the first local peach of the season brings an unexpected jolt of pleasure, like running into a friend you lost track of years ago. How extraordinary peaches taste—soft, fuzzy skin giving way to sweet, slippery pulp dripping with an almost tropical flavor. These sundaes showcase ripe peaches in all their glory.

1 cup sugar	Juice of ½ lemon
⅓ cup water	2 tablespoons rum
⅔ cup cream	½ cup salted peanuts
4 large, ripe peaches	2 pints vanilla ice cream

Combine sugar and water in a heavy saucepan. Stir over medium heat until sugar dissolves. With a wet pastry brush, remove any sugar crystals from sides of pan. Turn heat to high and boil until syrup turns a light amber, about 3 to 4 minutes. Remove from heat and whisk in cream a tablespoon at a time (mixture will foam). Set aside (caramel sauce may be chilled; warm slightly before serving).

Peel peaches and cut into slices. Place in a bowl and sprinkle with lemon juice; stir well. Sprinkle with rum. Chill.

Just before serving, stir peanuts into caramel sauce. Scoop ice cream into 4 serving dishes. Spoon peaches over ice cream. Top with the caramel-peanut sauce.

Makes 4 servings.

The Tips

Chapter 11
How to . . .

While writing this book, I kept thinking, "What will you need to know when you're on your own?" I feel like a mother sending a kid off to college.

In November you'll need to know how to roast a turkey, and at Christmas or Easter, how to cook a ham. In June you'll wonder how long to grill a slab of ribs.

That's how the "How To . . ." chapter came about. In it are the step-by-step guide to cooking a turkey that I wrote each November, the lowdown on different types of hams, info on cooking and eating a lobster and the very best ways to barbecue ribs and grill steaks, based on interviews with experts and years of testing. I've also included a few paragraphs on cooking chestnuts because someone asks every fall, and precise instructions for cooking boneless chicken breasts so they don't have the texture of shoe leather.

I know you could manage just fine without all this hand-holding, but I worry. Humor me.

And anyway, you never know when you'll move, leaving behind your turkey-cooking directions stapled to back of a cabinet door, as did one lady who called in a panic on Thanksgiving Eve. Now all the important cooking tips are here in one place. Just don't forget to pack this book.

Roast a Turkey

The hardest part of preparing a turkey is carrying it home from the store. Turkey is amazingly easy to roast. Basically, you place it in a shallow pan, shove it in the oven and forget about it for several hours. If you grease the turkey beforehand, you don't even have to baste.

Buying

Plan on about 1½ pounds per person, which will be enough for generous servings and leftovers the next day.

If you prefer a fresh turkey, order it in advance and pick it up the day before you plan to roast it. Fresh, raw turkeys should be refrigerated no longer than two days.

Thawing

Plan ahead. A 10-to-16-pound turkey takes three days to thaw in the refrigerator in its original wrapper, the recommended method of thawing.

If you forget, use the quick-soak method. Place the turkey, in its original wrapper, in a sink and fill with cold water. Change the water every 30 minutes to prevent it from warming up and posing food-poisoning problems. Allow 30 minutes per pound. Do not thaw your turkey at room temperature.

Preparing

Just before you're ready to put the turkey into the oven, remove the original wrapping and remove the packets of neck and giblets from the body and neck cavities. Wash the bird inside and out, and pat dry the outside.

Stuff the turkey. This is easy to do if you upend the turkey in a large bowl. Spoon the stuffing into the body cavity. The neck cavity may be stuffed, also. Don't pack down the stuffing, because stuffing expands during cooking.

Figure on about one-half cup stuffing per pound for turkeys under 10 pounds, and three-fourths cup for larger birds.

Do not stuff the bird the evening before Thanksgiving, or even an hour before roasting. To prevent bacteria from growing in the stuffing, stuff the turkey immediately before you pop it into the oven. The stuffing itself may be made a day in advance and refrigerated in a plastic bag or bowl, though.

Truss (or not)

Some turkeys come with wire holders or folds of turkey skin that truss the birds—that is, hold in the legs to retain the shape and prevent the stuffing from falling out.

If your turkey has no such contraption, there are a number of ways to make do. The easiest way is to tie the legs together with string, and wedge a slice of bread in the opening of the body cavity to keep the stuffing in place.

Trussing needles and skewers are available in housewares shops if you want to get fancy.

Roasting

Place the bird, breast-side up, in a shallow roasting pan.

The sides of the pan should be no more than 2 or 3 inches deep. A high-sided roasting pan will shield the thighs, which take the longest to cook. By the time the thighs are done, the breast will be overcooked.

Rub the turkey all over with butter or margarine. Roast it, uncovered, at 325 degrees until brown. Only then should you cover the turkey loosely with aluminum foil. If you cover the turkey sooner, or cover it tightly, you will be baking your turkey instead of roasting it. The skin will be soft and pale instead of crisp and brown. Basting is not necessary, as the juices do not penetrate the meat.

Determining doneness

The best way to tell when a turkey is done is with a meat thermometer. Insert it in the thickest part of the thigh, but not touching the bone. The turkey is done when the thermometer registers 180 to 185 degrees.

An alternate method is to prick the thigh with a fork. The turkey is done when the juices run clear. Don't rely on those plastic, pop-up thermometers embedded in some turkeys. They won't tell you when the thigh is done, and that's what is important. Also, the pop-up thermometers don't always pop up at the correct time.

Forget what your mother told you about wiggling a turkey leg to tell when the bird is done. If the turkey leg wiggles easily, the turkey is beyond done. The breast meat probably tastes like cardboard at that point.

Serving

Allow the turkey to stand, tightly covered with foil, for 20 to 30 minutes before carving. This brings the juices to the surface and allows you to carve smooth slices. If you carve the turkey right from the oven, the meat will shred.

Remove all of the stuffing from the body and neck cavities before serving. Otherwise, bacteria could grow.

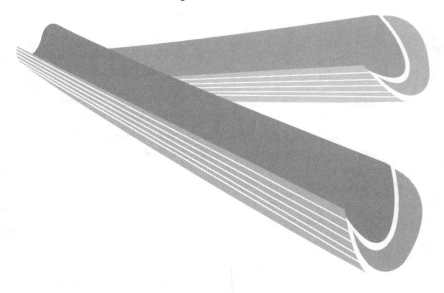

Cooking Chestnuts

....

To roast chestnuts for dicing or puréeing, roast no more than six at a time—a dozen if you have a helper.

....

Either cut an `X' in the flat side with a paring knife, or saw a ring around the chestnut with a serrated knife. (The serrated blade on a Swiss Army knife works great.)

Roast the chestnuts on a cookie sheet at 375 degrees for 6 to 8 minutes. If you roast them longer, the skin will stick.

Peel the chestnuts immediately, holding the nuts in dish towels to protect your fingers. Then start on the next batch.

If you're roasting chestnuts in a fireplace, the small, domestic chestnuts will do. For recipes, buy large, Italian chestnuts. The small chestnuts would work, but peeling them by the pound would be tedious.

After oven-roasting and peeling, the chestnuts must be cooked further for use in recipes. An easy way to finish cooking them is to simmer the chestnuts in water to cover for about 20 to 30 minutes or until soft but not mushy.

Make Great Barbecued Ribs

Cooking decent barbecued ribs need not be complicated. We've heard of aficionados who smoke their ribs for 12 hours, stir cough syrup into their sauce and build their fires in gussied-up, 55-gallon drums. That's fine if you want to make a career of barbecuing. But you don't really need all that hoopla to turn out excellent ribs. The following tips will make your ribs rock:

Meat

Despite what Texans say, the only meat worth its sauce is pork.

Ribs are sold in three basic cuts—spareribs, country-style ribs and baby back ribs. Spareribs are the most popular cut for barbecuing. They're less meaty than country or back ribs, but many rib-lovers believe that they are more flavorful.

Spareribs are cut from the rib cage of the hog. Whole slabs weigh from 2 to 5 pounds. The smaller the slab, the more tender the meat.

Country-style ribs aren't ribs at all. They are cut from the pork loin roast, the same cut of meat that produces pork chops. For country ribs, the roast is cut lengthwise into strips.

Baby back ribs come from the rib end of the pork loin roast. They're closer to the rib cage than country ribs, but are meatier than spareribs. Usually, they weigh less than 2 pounds per slab, which means they are unusually tender.

Sauce

Just about anything goes here. The only rule is to avoid basting the ribs until the last 10 minutes of cooking. If the sauce is slathered on sooner, it will burn and become bitter. Some rib-lovers don't baste at all, but serve the sauce on the side.

Regional sauce variations abound. In the Midwest, we like our sauce tomato- based and sweet.

Cooking

The method of cooking depends on how you like your ribs—falling-off-the-bone tender or rich and resilient. Fork-tender ribs are considered inferior by many barbecue experts. If you want tender, they reason, cook a pot roast.

The easiest routes to fork-tender ribs are to steam them over water in the oven or simmer them in sauce or another liquid for about 30 minutes before grilling. However, simmering leaches out much of the meat's flavor.

The classic way to barbecue ribs is long and slow, over indirect heat in a covered grill. This method produces meat that is rich and resilient, slightly firm to the bite but not tough.

The coals should be started well in advance, so that they are totally covered with ash and do not flare up when the meat is added.

Bank the coals to one side of the grill. Sprinkle a handful of wood chips over the coals. The chips should be soaked beforehand in water, so that they smoke instead of burn. When the chips begin to smoke, place the ribs on the opposite side of the grill and cover with the grill lid. A 2½- to 4-pound slab of ribs will cook in about 1 to 1¼ hours. Scatter more wood chips over the coals from time to time during cooking. You may have to add an additional lump or two of charcoal to keep the heat going.

When cooked this way, the meat will become almost hamlike in texture and wonderfully smoky in flavor. You'll understand why some rib-lovers refuse to add sauce.

Choose & Bake a Ham

Knowing how hams are produced will help you sort out the varieties.

Naturally cured

Traditionally, hams were cured by burying them in salt, which drew out the moisture so they could be stored at room temperature without spoiling. Country hams still are cured this way. They are labeled merely "ham."

Chemically cured

Most supermarket hams are cured chemically, and must carry a different label. The best buy is the ham injected with the least amount of liquid. Look for "ham with natural juices" on the label, or the next best, "ham—added water."

Hams labeled "ham and water product" have the most liquid. They may be the least expensive per pound, but remember that you're paying for water at ham prices.

Smoked

After they're cured, some hams are smoked the old-fashioned way, by hanging them in a smokehouse over a smoldering fire. These hams are labeled "naturally smoked." You won't find many of them in supermarkets, though. Most commercial hams are chemically smoked by injecting them with a smoke-flavored solution.

Jane Snow Cooks

Canned

Most canned hams are boneless, which means—like boneless hams in the meat case—they have been made by pressing together large chunks of ham cut from the bone. Carefully read the label of a canned ham to see whether it must be refrigerated or whether it may be stored in the cupboard before the can is opened.

Boneless vs bone-in

Boneless and semiboneless hams are convenient, and an additional plus is that you aren't paying for a bone. But there's a trade-off, because bone-in hams are considered more flavorful.

Some people shy away from bone-in hams because they don't know how to carve them. Here's the secret: Slice the ham lengthwise, parallel to the bone.

Preparation

Whatever kind of ham you buy, unless it's canned or a ham slice, you will have to shave off the tough skin. Just slip a knife between the skin and the fat or the meat and slice it away. If your ham has a thick layer of fat, slice off all but one-fourth inch of fat.

Roasting

Fresh hams are uncooked hams that must be roasted, like a pork roast. But even fully cooked hams should be baked to bring out the flavor and kill any bacteria that may linger in the meat. A modern, chemically cured ham should be baked to an internal temperature of 160 degrees. Bake it uncovered at 325 degrees for about 15 minutes per pound.

The glaze should be brushed on the ham during the last 30 minutes of baking. Otherwise, the sugar in the glaze may burn.

Cook & Cut Up a Lobster

Cutting up a lobster takes about two minutes if you know what you're doing. Here's how:

Yank off both claws at the body with a twisting motion. Gently tap the claw shells in several places with a meat mallet or hammer to crack them, then peel off the shells and pull out the meat.

Twist the tail to remove it from the body. Wash off the green stuff, which are the inedible innards. Turn the tail upside down to expose the relatively soft underside. Cut it up the middle with kitchen scissors. While separating the shell slightly with one hand, pull out the meat in one piece with the other, much as you would unzip a zipper, starting at the fat end.

Throw away the main body and attached legs or save them to make a broth. The tiny legs each contain a shred of meat, but removing it is so tedious it would drive you nuts.

That's it. Then all you have to do is dip each morsel in melted butter.

If you're using the meat in a recipe, buy the lobster at a store that will cook it for you for free. Some supermarkets and seafood stores offer this service. Ask that the lobster be cooked for just 5 minutes. This will kill the lobster and partially cook the meat, allowing you to finish cooking it with your recipe.

If you prefer to cook the lobster yourself, buy it the same day you plan to use it, and store it in your refrigerator crisper, wrapped in damp paper towels. Don't create a swimming pool for your lobster in the bathtub, because fresh water kills lobsters.

Lobsters must be alive when they are cooked, and the livelier the better. Choose the lobster cavorting around the tank, not the one sitting lifeless on the bottom. If your stored lobster seems groggy and inert when you plunge him into the pot, check the tail after cooking. The tail of a live lobster will curl during cooking.

To cook a live lobster, plunge it headfirst into a large pot of boiling water and boil for about 15 minutes. Then cool and cut apart as outlined above.

Grill a Steakhouse-Quality Steak

Serious steak restaurants turn out crusty, juicy, full-flavored steaks that are hard to duplicate at home. Hard, but not impossible. Here are some tips from steak masters:

Buy thick steaks—at least 1 inch thick. Thick steaks cook much better than thinner steaks. To get a true steakhouse flavor, you must char the steak on the outside. Thinner steaks overcook when grilled in this manner. If a thick steak is too large for one person, split it after cooking.

Build a really hot fire. At home, it's hard to equal the intensity of the heat restaurants use. You can come close by building a large charcoal fire. Don't skimp on the coals. A big heap of coals should be arranged on one-half of the grill and allowed to burn for about a half-hour, until covered with ash. Pull some of the coals to the other side of the grill so that you have a pile of hot coals on one side, and a single layer on the other.

Sear the steaks over high heat, then cook them over low heat.

The steaks are placed on the grill over the big pile of hot coals. Sear them for about 2 minutes on each side, until the outside is a rich, deep brown.

With tongs (don't pierce the steaks with a fork and let the juices escape), move the steaks to the other side of the grill. Continue cooking, turning once, until they reach the desired degree of doneness.

A 1½-inch-thick steak (I experimented with both strip steak and filet mignon) will take about 7 minutes to cook to medium-rare, not counting the time it takes to sear. Those who like their steaks rare or medium-well should adjust the time downward or upward a minute or two.

If the coals flame at any time during grilling, douse the flames with a squirt bottle or move the steaks temporarily to another part of the grill until the flames subside.

You now have the perfect steak.

Produce Juicy, Tender Chicken Breasts

A fresh, properly cooked boneless breast bursts with juices and can be cut with a butterknife. If your chicken doesn't match that description, read on.

The most important thing you can do to ensure moistness is to buy fresh chicken that has never been frozen. That eliminates most of the chicken sold in supermarkets, which legally can be "hard chilled" to below freezing and still be labeled "fresh."

Buy chicken that has been shipped on ice rather than partially frozen for shipping. Poultry stores and a few supermarkets sell such chicken, and it is worth a special trip. The difference in moisture content after cooking is significant. Of course, don't freeze the chicken after you get it home, either. Buy just what you need and use it while still fresh.

The second way to ensure moist meat is to cook the boneless breasts either briefly or for a long time. There's no middle ground.

Because of the protein structure, chicken must be cooked either just until opaque (about 7 minutes over medium-high heat for boneless breasts), or long and slowly. In-between times of 10 to 30 minutes produce dry, tough chicken.

Sautéing over medium-high heat allows the interior to cook while the exterior browns and seals in the juices. About 3½ minutes per side is plenty.

Those determined to kill every last possible bacterium in the chicken may worry that 7 minutes isn't long enough, but it is. Make a cut in the thickest breast at the thickest part to make sure the meat is white all the way through. With practice, you'll be able to tell when the chicken is done by pressing the meat with your finger.

And remember than even a minute of overcooking will turn a tender piece of chicken into a tough bird.

Index

Pizza
  Cajun chicken, 178
  tomato-ciabatta, 71
  white, 162
Pork
  carne adovada, 95
  garlic in lettuce leaves, 68
  ham, choosing and baking, 214
  ham with gingersnaps, 176
  meatballs, tiny, 129
  pad Thai, 70
  prosciutto & grilled asparagus,
    121
  pulled, Yankee Carolina barbecue,
    160
  riblets, pineapple-ginger glazed,
    120
  ribs, Szechuan with hot chili oil,
    79
  tenderloin, pecan-crusted with
    honey-ginger sauce, 161
  Vietnamese, in lettuce leaves, 106
Potatoes
  mashed, garlic, 151
  salad, French with garlic & mint,
    149
  smashed, grilled, Roger's, 154
  sweet (See Sweet Potatoes)
Potato nests, 8
Pot roast, Pennsylvania, 74
Prosciutto. See Pork. See also Soup:
  fontina-prosciutto
Pudding
  bread, coconut-pecan, 196
  rice, white chocolate-sour cherry,
    204
Puffs, Gus', 21
Pumpkin pie, ultimate, 190

R
Radishes, sautéed, 144
Red velvet cake, 22
Restaurants. See names of individual
  restaurants
Ribs
  beef (See Beef)
  cooking, 213
  cuts, 212
  meat selection, 212

pork (See Pork)
sauce, 212
Rice, hot, 12
Rice noodles with beef and broccoli,
  stir-fried, 174
Roast beef, herbed in salt crust, 36
Roger's grilled smashed potatoes, 154
Rum cream pie, 14
Rum, hot buttered, 67
Russo, David, 145

S
Saint Nicolas Orthodox Church, 40
Salad
  bean (Nick Anthe's), 5
  bread, Tuscan (See Salad:
    panzanella)
  chicken, Persian, sandwiches, 84
  chicken, Vietnamese, 145
  endive, Belgian, with carrots &
    walnuts, 137
  panzanella, 139
  potato, French with garlic & mint,
    149
  salmon & new potato, 138
  spinach, orange & cashew, 140
  tomato, fried green 136
Salad dressing. See Dressings
Salmon & asparagus spring rolls, 114
Salmon & new potato salad, 138
Salsa, mango, 165
Samosas, 112
Sangria. See Beverages
Sauces
  bourbon, 197
  for kung bao shells, 109
  for Vietnamese pork in lettuce
    leaves, 107
  spicy orange, 115
  stir-fry, Szechuan, 76
  tomato, roasted 77
  uncooked (for cabbage rolls), 171
Sauerkraut balls, 39
Savage beast cheesecake, 48
Schellenbach, Pete, 139
Schneider, Moe, 175
Scones, blueberry, lemon-lavender,
  55
Sherman, Elaine, 64

White chili, 38
White chocolate banana cream pie, 100
White chocolate-sour cherry rice pudding, 204
Wings, chicken. *See* Chicken
Winter vegetable hash, 155

Y

Yankee Carolina pulled pork barbecue, 160

Z

Zgonc, Diane, 47

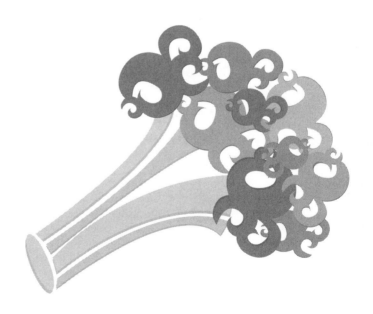

Ringtaw Books

Tara Kaloz, editor, *Our Boys in Blue and Gold: A Chronicle of Zips Football*

David Lee Morgan Jr., *High School Heroes: Athlete's Stories of Inspiration, Dedication, and Hope*

Jane Snow, *Jane Snow Cooks: Spirited Recipes and Stories*